live close to

HOME

PETER DENTON

RMB

RMB | Rocky Mountain Books Ltd.
rmbooks.com
@rmbooks
facebook.com/rmbooks

Cataloguing data available from Library and Archives Canada
ISBN 978-1-77160-182-5 (hardcover)
ISBN 978-1-77160-183-2 (electronic)

Printed and bound in Canada by Friesens

Distributed in Canada by Heritage Group Distribution and in the U.S. by Publishers Group West

For information on purchasing bulk quantities of this book, or to obtain media excerpts or invite the author to speak at an event, please visit rmbooks.com and select the "Contact Us" tab.

RMB | Rocky Mountain Books is dedicated to the environment and committed to reducing the destruction of old-growth forests. Our books are produced with respect for the future and consideration for the past.

We acknowledge the financial support of the Government of Canada through the Canada Book Fund and the Canada Council for the Arts, and of the province of British Columbia through the British Columbia Arts Council and the Book Publishing Tax Credit.

Contents

Preface

Make a list of words most used but least understood these days, and *sustainability* would be near
the top. The basic consensus would be that sustainability is a problem in a global consumer culture
where limitless human needs are pushing against
the boundaries of what the Earth can provide.

This is seen as a problem without any immediate or scalable solution. We talk about *taking steps*
toward sustainability, not *achieving* it. We want
to believe that small-scale efforts, like recycling
our plastic bottles, will make a difference, but set
against the general wastefulness of a throw-away
society, such efforts seem pointless. Success seems
only local or temporary. It is easier to turn a blind
eye, to pretend there is no problem at all, or to project the issues far enough into the future that sustainability becomes someone else's problem, not
ours.

Five years ago, I decided to tackle this problem of sustainability head-on, to find a middle course between denial and despair.

As a historian, I knew that global consumer culture had developed over time. I began with the assumption that sustainability is primarily a social and cultural problem, not a scientific or technological one, with roots (and therefore solutions) in society and culture. Those roots are Western, European and Judeo-Christian; the colonial empires of the past 500 years were hardly accidental and the social and cultural foundations they laid were obvious.

Yet trading, piracy, slavery, warfare – all the trappings of empire – were not new in 1500. In some form, they are found in every civilization on record. Something shifted in Western society and culture from the Renaissance onward, however, that changed the trajectory of how people viewed themselves, how they lived together and how they saw the world.

What were the crucial choices that so radically changed our perspective over the past 500 years and led us into an unsustainable future? What different choices could we make to change course or restore balance? What reasons do we have to be hopeful, that what we do will make a real difference for enough people – and in time?

My response to these questions led to a series of three books. This is the third. Each one deals with a different facet – they can be read separately, but together they are intended to make you think more clearly about your life, your world and your future.

The presumption is that once you think more clearly about these things, you will find your own reasons to live differently. You will then share that change in perspective with the people you care about and within your community.

In *Gift Ecology: Reimagining a Sustainable World* (2012), I identified a preoccupation with mechanism as both the foundation of the achievements of Western industrial culture and its Achilles' heel. The resulting imbalance, favouring the economics of exchange over the possibilities inherent in a gift, led directly to valuing everything (the Earth, other creatures and even ourselves) primarily in material and economic terms. We can't hope to solve the problem of sustainability by tweaking that game or playing it better – we need to change the game itself. Exchange needs to be balanced by gift, just as economy needs to be balanced by ecology, all within a universe of relations.

In *Technology and Sustainability* (2014), I developed the first book's prelude ("On Ethics, Technology and Sustainability") into a demonstration of how we can change the game. Sustainability may be a social and cultural problem, but technology is a critical element. Technology is a product of choices – it is neither accidental nor inevitable. We make choices for reasons and those reasons reflect our values, what we think is important. Technology, therefore, is in our heads, not our hands – it is instrumental or applied knowledge, knowledge we use to do something. It is definitely not new; it is present in every culture at every time. Every civilization develops the technology it needs to survive – or it doesn't survive.

You could say technology is what makes us human, but this also means technology is always under our control. We choose to develop and use it, every day – all of us, all the time. We can work back from examples of our technologies to identify the choices that led to their development and use – and then the reasons for those choices and the values behind the reasons. If we don't like the values we uncover, we have the power and the responsibility to change them – and consequently change our reasons, our choices and finally our technologies.

Changing course toward a sustainable future therefore requires us to make better choices today than we did yesterday – not necessarily great or amazing ones, just better ones, but made by all of us and not just a select few. History provides many examples of major shifts in society and culture that result from the choices of individuals rather than the actions of a group. We not only *need* to change the game, we *can* do it, just as it has been done before.

In the prelude to the second book ("Stories Around the Cultural Fire"), I observed that one of the oldest elements of culture is the story told around the communal fire, the moral story that passes values down from generation to generation and weaves the individual into community.

Today we may lack that communal fire, but we are still woven into community by moral stories that explain our place in the web of life. Our culture is unsustainable in part because the stories we have learned do not weave relationships between people and the Earth as they used to do. Our choices not only destroy the Earth but actually *de-story* it, which is far worse.

So I argued we need to change the story of our relationship to Technology from powerlessness to choice, from helplessness to responsibility. We need to understand and celebrate technology as the tool we use to create a better future, so long as our choices reflect values that sustain, renew and respect the Earth.

Gift Ecology is therefore about where we have come from, while *Technology and Sustainability* is about where we are going and how to get there. But there is still one more piece, one more facet, that needs to be developed: we need to understand what went so terribly wrong with our cultural story that we could become so alienated from each other and from the Earth.

Solving "the problem of sustainability" requires all of us to recognize something foundational to our experience of being human. It is only shared recognition and mutual understanding that will enable us to transcend the barriers of race, religion, ideology and culture that have become seemingly impossible obstacles to a sustainable future.

We need to go behind the story of how we live with each other and against the Earth today, to find and mend the broken threads and weave them into a new story for our generation and for those to come.

It is a large task for a small book, the last in what I have come to call the "Scrub Oak Trilogy." Like any good story, however, its size doesn't matter. It only needs to strike the right chord in the hearts – and minds – of the reader.

If it does, then please add your own threads to the telling and retelling of what, like the first two books, is offered to you here as a Gift.

❦

In *Technology and Sustainability*, I attempted to thank people whose influence has shaped my work through the various relationships we shared. It was a long list, but afterward I kept encountering others who should have been included.

Rather than repeat the same mistake here, I will only offer my appreciation to everyone who has struck a spark in my life, from the familiarity of friends to the casual conversation of strangers.

Without those sparks, it would be a cold and barren existence. With them, anything is possible!

For their patience, love and support at home (where much of my writing is done these days), I especially appreciate Mona, Ruth and Daniel.

With this third manifesto, Don Gorman and his staff at Rocky Mountain Books have closed the circle that began with the email I sent him out of the blue in January 2012. Ideas are the levers we need to shift the world – but without the words to express those ideas and without the books to communicate those words, nothing much happens. Thank you for all that you do and for the wisdom behind it.

Finally, this book needs a dedication. For reasons that will emerge more clearly by the end, a book entitled *Live Close to Home* could only be dedicated to my mother, June Smith Denton. With tenacity, and overcoming obstacles of all sorts, she has made "home" her life's work, to the comfort of more people than she knows.

St. Andrews, Manitoba

Argument

Over the past decade, a consensus has emerged that sustainability is a social and cultural problem, not a scientific or technological one. Beyond the obvious markers of excess that characterize Western-style consumer societies, however, there is much less consensus about how to shift choices and lifestyles in a more sustainable direction.

To step over the philosophical mire and avoid sinking into the debate over what sustainability means, I want to take a more pragmatic approach in this book.

Whatever success local sustainability initiatives have had, it has not so far proven to be scalable to the extent that global transformation requires. Nor are individual lifestyle changes occurring at the rate that rapidly approaching planetary boundary conditions demand. We need to identify and change fundamental underlying characteristics of our culture in order to make such transformation possible – and for it to happen in time. These characteristics are best described as values, however, not as behaviours – the values that lie behind certain choices instead of others.

Focusing only on sustainable production and consumption masks a significant issue: that the majority of the global population has to produce and consume *more*, not *less*, to survive in a climate-changing world. At the same time, we also need to affirm and enhance those values that allow necessary development to be sustainable, without repeating on a larger scale (and in a more fragile climate situation) the mistakes that Western industrial culture has made over the past 500 years.

One of the core values in both circumstances is proximity – what is nearby. I argue that the development of Western industrial culture depended upon the devaluation of the proximity that had previously always marked human social activity. As this new culture developed, less importance was placed on what was "local." As we chose to live further and further from "home," our lives as individuals and as citizens became increasingly unsustainable.

By exploring six different facets of what it means to "live close to home," I will demonstrate why proximity is a crucial determinant of a sustainable society. To say this in plainer language, we have to stop preferring the far away over what is close at hand, in time and in space. Otherwise, a global culture of "sustainability" will not be possible, nor will any further development anywhere be sustainable.

⚜

If the roots of Western industrial culture are to be found in the Renaissance period in Europe, as I argued in *Gift Ecology*, its second label as the Age of Discovery is a telling example of how the horizons of European society expanded in the 15th century. Whether the discovery was of new lands, new peoples or new sources of wealth to be gained by exploitation or trade, the medieval underpinnings of a relatively stable, local, agrarian society were weakened. By the end of the 18th century, such stability was gone, succeeded by the upheavals of revolution and war on both sides of the Atlantic Ocean.

For the "discovered" peoples, no aspect of these incursions by strangers from away was good news for the local economy or for local well-being.

Catastrophic social and cultural changes occurred, along with death from epidemic diseases on a scale far beyond Europe's own experience of the Black Death 200 years earlier.

For the "discoverers," however, there were also serious social and cultural problems. The benefit of sending undesirables or surplus populations "away" from the home country was offset by the effects of windfall wealth "from away" that devalued land back home through inflation. Whether the wealth was precious metals from the silver mines of the New World or new trade goods that commanded high prices, the centre of economic gravity shifted away from land holdings in Europe to sources of offshore wealth.

These sources of wealth were made more tenuous by the distances involved, the reliability of technology used for transport (such as ships navigating by guess instead of by longitude) and the political and economic implications of protecting this revenue at all points along the way. Piracy became an instrument of state policy because it was cheaper and easier to steal the money from someone else than it was to earn it.

New lands, new places, new adventures, escape

from daily drudgery – "it's a pirate's life for me" came to distinguish Renaissance culture from its medieval precursor. Those new places could be in the heavens, as Galileo's telescope revealed mountains on the moon and new moons altogether, or they could be in a drop of pond water, as van Leeuwenhoek's microscope revealed new creatures too small for the human eye.

Whether or not it was possible for most people to break out of their current situation and head for the New World, that potential for adventure became part of the cultural vernacular. "Away" had been an option before, but it had not been linked to a reasonable chance of returning laden with pieces o' eight or of surviving long enough to send reports back home of a new life in distant lands flowing with milk and honey.

As these new sources of wealth "from away" shifted the balance of power in the European states from landholders and the agrarian economy, new opportunities emerged for Europeans socially disadvantaged by their traditional culture. The adage that "knowledge was power" became embodied in emerging technologies, to the point that by the mid-19th century the captains of industry far outweighed the landlords of yesteryear in terms of money and influence.

Further, colonial empires depended on "away" for sources of raw materials and for captive markets for domestic manufactured goods. What mattered most was the store of wealth created by the transactions, not the conditions in which the raw materials were produced abroad or the conditions at home in which the goods were manufactured. Whether that wealth was measured in dollars and cents or in pounds and shillings, measured it was – and as ruthlessly as the circumstances required.

By the time of the Second Industrial Revolution of the 1850s, these imperial and industrial patterns of production and consumption were well established. Where revolution did not occur first, some of the most self-destructive excesses of earlier centuries were addressed through legislation, the rise of trade unions and other initiatives in diplomacy and government.

Yet the lure of the exotic continued to be reflected in the cultural vernacular on both sides of the Atlantic. The frontier mentality was as likely to be found in Africa as in the United States, as wagon trains and gunboats pushed further into uncharted and therefore "undiscovered" territory waiting to be civilized and exploited for wealth that otherwise would be left untapped. Dealing with the locals was either amusing or hazardous, but it was all part of shouldering "the white man's burden" in faraway places.

The realization that discovery depended significantly on science and technology also fuelled a collective desire for something new and different. In the Age of Power (as the 19th century may be called, with the advent of the steam engine, internal combustion and electricity), there was no question about the changes wrought by inventions and their application – nor of their ultimate economic value.

The factory system, leading into mass production techniques, fundamentally changed the availability of quality goods at reasonable prices for the bulk of Western populations. The expansion and growth of Western culture in the 20th century was twice tempered by the devastation of war on an industrial scale, but each time it recovered, rebounded and extended its reach to what we are now starting to recognize as the limits imposed by planetary boundaries.

In terms of our needs (and wants), however, the discussion of limits is too often greeted with resistance and rejection. As citizens of a global consumer culture, our patterns of production and consumption are so far from sustainable that they more accurately reflect the absurd slogan of the *Toy Story* character Buzz Lightyear: "To infinity... and beyond!"

From medieval to Renaissance and then to industrial cultures, what was distant in time or space caught the fancy of the individuals responsible for the choices that led to these ultimately unsustainable situations. It is not as simple as the "ancients versus moderns" debates that have occurred since the 1500s. The near at hand, the close, the familiar, were seen to be less interesting and therefore inherently less valuable than the mysterious or distant.

The maxim that "a bird in hand is worth two in the bush" ceased to have relevance for those much more interested in what else the bush might contain. Certainly popular culture celebrated those who returned with whatever they found as a result of taking risks. "Fortune favours the brave" – and it was clear there was nothing brave about staying close to home and tending to the familiar, however

8

much (in reality) such caution was normally rewarded.

Simply stated, in the hierarchy of values that lie behind individual choices, proximity was displaced from the rank it had always held in human social interactions, both practical and psychological. The result has been the increasingly unsustainable character of Western industrial culture, which has since spread around the world.

Stating the problem may be the first step to any solution, but it is no solution. If living "far away" is the problem, if proximity has been devalued in favour of something distant from us in time and space – physical and psychological – then the solution must lie in reversing that tendency.

It is hardly original to lobby for the local – sustainability advocates have been talking about "locavores" for some time. There are many groups telling us what we should do, whether that means "transitioning" in local communities or compounding everything into a single great transformation of global culture.

While the advice may be sound and capable of changing individual behaviours, the programs I have seen so far always founder on their inability to bridge cultural, generational, social, economic, religious and other divides. What works for one group in one place for one set of reasons will either fail outright or fail to convince another group somewhere else at some other time.

Without the right moral story in which to embed the relevant lessons, I argue, such failure is inevitable. There are too many other narratives that pull us in the wrong direction and thus perpetuate the unsustainable global culture we now all share.

To counter this, each community needs its own moral story, its own way of linking its identity to the values, reasons and choices a sustainable future requires. There will obviously be similarities in the outcomes, because we share common basic needs and circumstances, but the reasons for choosing those outcomes could vary wildly between different communities.

What matters, in the end, is the moral of the whole story – not the characters, nor even the plot.

🦟

Complexity is at the heart of our inability to create a consensus of what to do, to move beyond analysis of problems and into an ethical framework of what should be done, how and why – and by whom.

The struggle to articulate the United Nations Sustainable Development Goals, which were finally approved in the fall of 2015, involved more players, more countries, more civil society engagement, than any such global initiative had ever managed to include. The process was tortuous, the selections of goals and targets often acrimonious, leaving the outcomes of some debates more ambiguous than ideal.

In an environment of policy summaries, sound bites and quick briefings, how can we manage global complexity in a coherent and functional manner, communicating intentions, plans and outcomes across linguistic, social and cultural barriers?

The application of method helps only so far. Method underpinned the rapid and extraordinary development of Western industrial culture, but it requires a linearity of focus, a mechanical mindset, that drives in only one direction.

So we make lists – even lists of sustainable development targets and goals! – and only then realize how many things appear on several different lists. These are then labelled "cross-cutting issues," to be dealt with once we have gone through everything else.

Such analytical methods are incredibly powerful, but only to a point. When they attempt to describe the dynamics of interrelated complex systems, even the label of "cross-cutting issue" is inadequate. A list of such issues is even less helpful, because it tries to provide a linear depiction of things that, by nature, are not linear.

It is not original to call for "system thinking." And despite the best of intentions, more problems arise when we try to define the "systems" we are "thinking" about. If attempts to define sustainability risk sucking us into philosophical mire, "system thinking" risks circling a black hole into which good ideas vanish with nothing more than a momentary flash of light.

Instead, I am going to retreat into ancient cosmology and offer my thoughts within a series of concentric spheres, spheres that have no specific boundary as we move in and out of the centre, which is located in who we are as individuals. We need to listen for the harmony in the music of the spheres, because when there is no harmony, only dissonance, bad things start to happen.

What happens in my yard in Manitoba may well affect butterflies in Australia, but I have no way of understanding the causality involved. But I can understand how the things I do affect the world around me, moving out in concentric circles (or spheres) like the ripples from a pond into which I have dropped the proverbial stone.

So, as a good Methodist (in the nonreligious sense), I have provided below my list of six common themes to be explored: food, knowledge, reality, community, economy and ecology. These give us a framework for understanding how to reverse the damage that distance has done to our world, our communities and ourselves. The six themes make an equally good list of what to emphasize to avoid exporting the mistakes of Western industrial culture to other places. Those themes are divided into two sets, the first of which creates an inner sphere and the second of which creates an outer sphere.

In each of these six instances, it will be clear that the problems have arisen because of the way we have chosen *not* to live "close to home." Reverse those choices, reverse those decisions, and we reverse those negative effects. Our systems then will also reverse course, toward a more sustainable future than the one that otherwise, surely, will soon be upon us all.

Our individual choices can never finally be dictated or coerced by someone else – or required by governments of any kind. Like the thread tied to the nose of an elephant, however, they can be guided by a good story that makes us want to go in the right direction.

Stories of various kinds – myths and parables, for example – have always been the way that humans have managed the problems of complexity in a universe of dynamic relations. There is always music in a story people remember, just as lyrics make tunes into songs.

I hope what you read below will nurture a story that grows in the telling – or a tune that spreads in the sharing.

✺

As in the other two books in the Scrub Oak Trilogy, there are two parts, with three chapters in each. To continue the musical analogy, they are the inner and outer spheres, framed by a Prelude and a Postlude and paused for thought in the middle by an Interlude.

Prelude
Four Words of Power

Four words to change the world: Live close to home.

We have increasingly emphasized the global village over the village in which we live. Whatever the arguments in support of globalization, our preference for the far away at the expense of what is close to home is at the heart of the environmental and social catastrophes that, some days, seem utterly unavoidable.

If we live close to home, if we focus on changing and improving the aspects of our lives over which we have control, the system effects of such a transformation can only be positive.

It is so simple, it must be wrong. Given the complex problems that confront us in our generation, the answers cannot be summed up in such a simple phrase.

Yet complexity is precisely the root of those problems. We have created more and more complicated human systems – systems that now circle the globe – without a solid understanding of how these systems affect the larger planetary systems within which they are embedded.

Complexity, experts and impossible scenarios dominate our horizons these days, provoking despair instead of hope. They close the door to a sustainable future instead of tearing down the walls that prevent us from seeing the world as it is – with all its dangers, perhaps, but also with all its possibilities.

On the one hand, the apostles of Gaia – those who see the Earth acting like a single organism, with all its systems in balance – predict a global catastrophe that eradicates the excess humans who, like hostile bacteria, have done so much damage. On the other hand, the disciples of Commerce – those who consider money to be the measure of everything – take the Earth for granted, a perpetual source of profit that only needs to be managed more efficiently for the benefit of humans in general and themselves in particular.

Most of us fall in between, bombarded with

information we don't understand, listening to duelling experts who predict the end of the world in one breath and then advise us on our long-term investments in the next.

Because we can't understand more than a little of the complex problems in the news, and because we feel that as individuals we have no power to change anything ourselves, we trudge through our daily lives, pretending through our actions that it is business as usual while actually worrying about what lies ahead.

As we struggle to keep food on the table or to give our children what they need (or want) today, we simply can't deal with the idea that the world we know might disappear. The tomorrow for which we are preparing ourselves and our children threatens to become more and more like a fantasy.

No matter how much we pretend or explain away the evidence that bombards us every day, in our hearts we know the dream is threatening to become a nightmare and we are powerless to stop it.

So, four simple words to change the world: Live close to home.

These words don't tell us which experts are right. They don't tell us "don't worry, be happy, everything's going to be fine." They also don't tell us to despair, that there is no hope for tomorrow.

These words tell us to focus on what we can do ourselves, where we live, for ourselves and for our children, for our community, right now. These four words are words of power, requiring us to accept the responsibility for what is going on in our own backyard – and to do something about it.

Live close to home – that's what sustainability is all about. When we try to live somewhere else, when what we mean by "home" depends on people and influences and materials from somewhere else, then we create a system that is ultimately unsustainable.

It is our local environment – physical, emotional, social and spiritual – that keeps us alive and healthy. When we get distracted from what is going on in our local area and focus instead on something or someone at a distance, we lose sight of the things we need in order to be healthy ourselves.

To be clear, this is not a self-help book. It is a reflection on what has gone wrong with our society and with us as individuals, in the larger context of a planet in crisis, because we have not been living close to home. By identifying the problems clearly, without shrinking from what they are, we have the best chance of making the decisions that can turn destructive systems into ones that instead give life. Living close to home restores our ability to change the future that otherwise is prepared for us by forces over which we are told daily we have no control. If you understand what "live close to home" means, in all of its dimensions, then put the book down. If you don't, then the observations here – as simple as they may be – are in combination perhaps the most important message you need to hear.

"Save the Planet" seems like the kind of thing you see on a placard during a protest march, something so large that the average person can't begin to understand what it means. And yet, if we consider the problems we can see in so many places, "Destroy the Planet" is an equally large concept, and we have been doing quite a good job of it over the past century or so.

The argument I make throughout this book is that we don't need complicated ideas or new technologies to save the planet (and ourselves along with it). What we need is understanding and the will to make the changes that need to be made at a local level. We need to apply the best of our ingenuity, our ability and the tools we already have to manage what happens close at hand. We need a new story, one that brings people to a consensus about how to live with each other and with the Earth, as we huddle around the global cultural fire. We need to understand what it means to "live close to home."

What control we have is over the here and now; the further we get from the here and now, the less control we have over what will happen. In all things, we need to eat with a shorter spoon.

Speaking of eating, to anchor the rest of the book in the reality of the everyday, close-at-hand, we might as well begin with food....

PART I

The Inner Spheres

Chapter 1
Food

"It tastes just like pickerel!" my son said. He had sampled some fish at our local grocery store and persuaded his mother to take home a package of the frozen fillets. When he handed me the package to put away and cook sometime in the future, I found it hard to believe that something frozen would taste that good. Pickerel, a freshwater fish found about 50 miles away in Lake Winnipeg and other northern waters, is a delicacy.

When I pulled it out of my freezer, I discovered to my chagrin that it was a wild fish called a Cape Capensis, caught off the coasts of South Africa and frozen a full year before. Much heavier and denser than pickerel, it was tasty, but it illustrated the problem with long-distance food today. Rather than bringing fish thousands of miles to eat that tasted "just like pickerel," we could have had frozen fish from 50 miles away that, well, *was* pickerel.

Every family has stories about food. My mother grew up poor in Nova Scotia during the war years and remembers eating so many tomato sandwiches in the fall at school that she still can hardly face one. A friend grew up in a community of lobster fishers in New Brunswick, where lobster was such common food that old claws were chew toys for the children.

Lobsters now travel, so even prairie supermarkets have a tank where dubious examples lurk, fed to consumers who have never seen them fresh in the wild thousands of miles away. Tomatoes arrive on our salads and in our sandwiches without fail – it is the rare consumer who notices where they happen to come from this month. Nor is taste much of a factor for those who have never picked them fresh off the vine.

Examples of changes in North American diets are easy to find. Members of the wartime generation who grew up outside of Florida will remember the Christmas orange, exotic and rare – a real treat of fresh citrus. These days, oranges are a sliced garnish often ignored at the side of the breakfast plate.

In an earlier generation, my grandmother's first taste of chocolate came in the middle of the Great War, when, as an 8-year-old, she shattered an arm. Her father, the station agent in a rural New Brunswick community, persuaded a railway contact to get him a small box of chocolates for a child who might not recover.

Today, however, children in North America expect oranges year-round and chocolate bars in steady supply, regardless of the point of origin (Florida, China or Ghana) and unaware of the journey between the source and the place of purchase.

It is the same with all the other usual suspects in our diet. When we go to the store, the price, quality and source might vary, but we expect to find the foods we want. News of a regional crop failure due to drought, flood or insects might produce a clucking of tongues, but no one expects the shelves to be empty come winter.

This leads me to the first example of how proximity has been demoted in Western culture and why it must be reclaimed as a crucial value: people have never before been so far removed from their food in terms of time, distance and knowledge as they are today.

We eat food with its origins in the past, from places we can't identify and about which we know very little before it ends up on our grocery store shelves. Prepared, precooked and virtually predigested, missing micronutrients and hiding microtoxins, the empty calories we eat promote obesity, induce disease and (most absurdly) create malnutrition in the midst of abundance.

There should be nothing closer to us than what we put in our mouths, what we eat, and yet it is the lack of proximity, the disregard of what is nearby, that leads to all of these problems.

While it is hard to convince North Americans of this reality, we are moving into a time when most of the world's population – including ourselves – is "food insecure." We do not have sufficient local control over the staple foods in our diets. We are unsure of what our food contains. We find it increasingly difficult to choose foods for a healthy lifestyle because it seems we are only choosing between unavoidable evils.

To be sure, some foods have always travelled a long distance. Some of the earliest discoveries of ancient trade goods have included spices, in particular, that made long journeys from exotic places to their destinations. These were small and easily carried, able to be preserved for the distance and time they travelled – and likely worth more than their weight in gold. In every sense, such items were a treat.

Staples were found much closer to home – a staple food, by definition, is something close to home, in sufficient quantity and regular supply to be a reliable source of food in the longer term. Lobsters might have been a staple in Nova Scotia, just as shrimp were in Louisiana and deer at one time in Kentucky – even buffalo (bison) in Manitoba and cod in Newfoundland – but elsewhere, out of their usual, natural habitat, all of these staple foods were luxuries.

Take a look in your cupboards and refrigerator and figure out the staple foods in your own diet today. Then find out their source, and you will be surprised at the distance your staple foods have travelled to feed you. When the food is processed or manufactured (as much of our staples are, instead of being grown or raised or hunted or harvested), find out not only where it was "made" but also where it was processed and where the ingredients in these manufactured foods originated.

When I was growing up in Manitoba, winter was a sparse time for fresh fruits and vegetables. There were oranges, lemons and grapefruit from Florida and bananas from points further south. Apples (Golden Delicious, Spartans or McIntosh) were poor, despite the price, looking as though they had rolled downhill from the Okanagan. Browning head lettuce, doubtful cucumbers and rock-hard tomatoes from California rounded out the picture, with onions, carrots and potatoes likely local but kept in cold storage as long as possible.

Today there are fresh things year-round. People disparage the quality of green beans in the cold of a February day, complaining when the tropical starfruit is not as good this week. When we go into the produce section, not only is the item we want available, we expect it to look good, too.

Our food system encourages this level of expectation, and not just for foods from the tropics. After all, Canadian wheat and other grains travel further than the farmers who grow them. They are often traded internationally several years after they are grown. This insulates consumers and markets alike from the effects of any particular year's disasters, while divorcing our customers from the reality of their food supply, just as we are from our own.

Long-distance food therefore leaves us vulnerable to whatever disrupts the system of just-in-time delivery. Do some research into what the supply of food might be in your area at any point in the year and you will realize how little (even grain) is actually stockpiled or kept in inventory these days. Whatever we need, including most of our staple foods, is delivered just in time. In many places, while the official numbers are usually kept quiet to prevent any panic, that supply may be as little as seven days.

Whether a natural supply crisis might be caused by floods, drought or natural disaster, or a delivery problem by strikes, terrorist attack or outbreak of epidemic disease – or even the high cost of transportation – never before have so many people been in such a precarious position simply because of the distance their food must travel from producer (or manufacturer) to consumer. Nor is the so-called 100-mile diet much of an alternative, as few of us would willingly walk 100 miles for our food.

This food insecurity is a fairly recent development. Not too many years ago, much of the population of North America lived on the farm or in rural communities surrounded by farms, or derived its income directly from the agricultural sector.

Even in the city, vegetable gardens were the norm; recipes were exchanged; produce was preserved by canning, pickling, drying or freezing. What was not grown in your garden came from close enough that, should you choose, you could visit the poultry farm, the hog barns, the beef ranch and the dairy farm. Food "from away" was available but tended to be fruits not grown locally. Canned, frozen or manufactured foods were expensive and outside the budgets of many families as anything more than an occasional treat. Much of what is now regarded as a "staple" food was until recently an optional, seasonal or luxury item.

As late as the 1960s, Winnipeg Hydro, the local utility company, would print a 20-page canning guide in the fall and deliver it free to every household in the city, just to ensure everyone understood the proper way to preserve foods for the winter.

How much of a difference a few decades can

make! Vegetable gardens are scarce in urban areas. Hard-earned family lessons in preserving food have not been passed along to the next generation, for whom the microwave, not the canner, is the ultimate kitchen necessity. We not only don't know where our food comes from, we also don't know how to cook it properly once it arrives.

⚜

Forty years ago, I lived with my family outside the city of Winnipeg, in rural St. Andrews, which then was in transition from farming area to commuter community. We had what we thought was a large garden – certainly lots of weeds for the kids to pull! – but in it we grew enough food to eat during the summer and to harvest, freeze, can and pickle vegetables for the winter. I will always remember the huge piles of green and yellow beans cooling on the counter after being put through the blancher – and just how many pea pods had to be shelled to put a few small bags into the freezer.

Tomatoes were canned, dill pickles, relish, jams and jellies – there seemed to be a variety that my own diet lacks today. Our carrots lasted until late fall, potatoes the same and onions a little longer – all without a root cellar, so we relied on the grocery store for these things over the winter. These staples might have come from more than 100 miles away, but not by much.

Every other year, we got bushels of small apple crabs (a backwards cousin of the crabapple) that were turned into jelly and apple pies by the dozens. Rhubarb was a constant, and raspberries and strawberries were picked at local farms in years when our own plants did not produce enough. We had gooseberries, currants, plums – and bought wild blueberries from vendors by the side of the highway.

Eggs came from the people next door. Milk was delivered from the dairy in Winnipeg, rain or shine – and all these years later, I still get a Christmas card from Bill the Milkman, long since retired.

We picked up the meat on Sundays after church from the butcher in Selkirk. Cheese was local, too. There were enough opportunities to buy or exchange things in the community so that we had more various foods than the ones we made ourselves.

With five kids, restaurant meals still happened often enough that we knew how to eat in public, but otherwise the cooking was done from scratch – and dishes washed up by hand.

To be sure, there was less global content in the food we ate. Spices, coffee and tea certainly came from away, just as they had for the past 150 years in the Red River settlement (though we grew and dried a number of our own herbs). We got canned foods from a distance (at a premium), trickling in to tempt the local cooks to try more exotic recipes.

Yet these were luxuries, treats, not the everyday food that steamed out of kitchens at the hands of cooks who contributed to the community dinners every fall, where hundreds if not thousands ate their fill from tables piled high with locally grown, home-cooked food.

If my father ever travelled to Nova Scotia, he always came back with a carton of lobsters packed in dry ice. I remember my grandmother's last visit to see us in Manitoba, when she was in her 90s. She got off the airplane and was trundled through to the baggage area in a wheelchair. We all greeted her warmly – and then left her to collect the two big boxes of lobster she had couriered for us from the Halifax airport!

Lobsters were not a staple on the Prairies but

were certainly a treat. They had to be cooked alive so that they would not become tainted. I remember once putting them on the concrete patio to be sure they were okay – and having to chase one sturdy specimen who made a fast break for the east coast and safety.

All creatures have an instinct for survival, a sense of optimism found in seizing the possibilities of the moment – even a lobster that wakes up on the Prairies.

⁂

However precarious the situation might be here, local communities in other parts of the world are even more vulnerable and food insecure because of how much food and other products they grow for export rather than local consumption. To the effects of climate change on weather patterns, including drought and desertification, add the decreasing productivity of overused agricultural land – compounded by rapid population growth and frequent political instability – and mass starvation is just over the horizon in parts of Africa and Asia.

This leads into the conundrum posed by industrial agriculture, both for sustainable development and for a sustainable future: How are we going to feed the world? Given the fourfold increase in population over the past century, on a planet that remains the same size, where are we going to get the food we need?

The assumption – or better yet, the presumption – is still that industrial agriculture is necessary to produce sufficient food to feed these seven billion people. This belief led directly to the Green Revolution of the 1970s and 1980s, with a substantial increase in productivity due to the use of intensive farming techniques, chemical fertilizers, pesticides and herbicides.

It worked marvellously – in the short term. In the medium term, yields have fallen, land has become exhausted, irrigation with groundwater has salinated soils to the point of sterility, pests have become resistant and global markets have come to dominate local production decisions. In the long term, intensive industrial agriculture is simply not sustainable, certainly not on the planetary scale necessary to feed the world.

The choice, then, is whether we continue to try and feed the world this way or whether we support, develop and maintain sustainable agriculture. It becomes a problem in system thinking, in system design. Estimates, for example, of the amount of food currently produced that is wasted at some point (on the journey from farm to fridge to fork) range as high as 40 per cent.

The reasons for food waste vary, depending on regional issues (from picky eaters who want pretty vegetables in one place, to a lack of refrigerated storage in another), but conservatively this wasted food would be enough to feed close to a billion people, every year. Add to this the problems in distribution and over-consumption (in countries where obesity is a growing problem) and the billions who are food insecure and hungry where they live could have more to eat than they do at the present – again, without increasing overall production.

The combination of malnutrition and too many calories results from the simple fact that Nature is better at agro-chemistry than any of the multinational corporations that try to manipulate and control what seeds are planted and what chemicals must be sprayed on the fields. It is one of the bitter ironies of our century that these efforts are labelled "scientific" when, in fact, they are often driven by market pressures rather than solid evidence, wise methods and much-needed humility in the face of the complexities of organic systems.

Living close to home when it comes to food requires us not to feed the world but to develop sustainable agriculture within the local contexts where we live. It requires us to have a local diet comprised of staple foods over which we have control, not the coerced uniformity of a global diet that ignores seasons and circumstances and delivers our staple foods just in time, from a distance.

Food can be (and is) grown in urban areas, which could also intentionally develop and support sustainable agriculture in the surrounding region. Distance needs to be factored into cost, eliminating the subsidies that make it cheaper to import food than grow it close to home and that foster an export market instead of feeding the people who grow the food.

The calories from industrial agriculture may be calculated in barrels of oil, because of the energy-intensive methods used in everything from fertilizers to the machinery required to farm the land and finally to transport the food to consumers at a distance. Given the serious implications of global warming on farming everywhere – and especially in developing countries – reducing greenhouse gas emissions and using agricultural methods that fix carbon dioxide, rather than spew it into the atmosphere, should be obvious choices to make.

Much of the world's food is still produced by smallholder farmers, whose interests and concerns are far different from those of farmers working on an industrial scale. Food security and sustainable development require a system into which all the means of production, everywhere, may be incorporated.

In the end, we don't have a hundred-mile diet. Our actual diet is an arm's length away. If we can't reach our food with our own hands, we need help to avoid starvation.

⚜

Local food requires personal choices close to home, however.

The apple orchards of the Annapolis Valley in Nova Scotia were plowed under during the 1960s because it was cheaper to bring in more uniform apples (in fewer varieties) from the United States. When this happened, something was lost, not just to the local area but to the Earth itself.

When I lived in southern Ontario, I made friends with a family that, decades before, had decided to start their own orchard. Over the years, on top of their day jobs in the steel mill, they added acre after acre of apple trees, nurturing species that had themselves been plowed under in the Niagara region.

From those apples came fresh cider in the fall, then pies and finally a shop where their produce and other local items could be sold. I enjoyed apples I did not know existed, learned that the Northern Spy apples were great for making apple pie but did not store well in the long term, that Mutsus were different from Russets – and to apologize when all we had left to cook with were lowly McIntoshes. I watched apples that fell to the ground before harvest being turned into cider – and realized these ground apples were better quality by far than the ones I had grown up eating at home on the Prairies.

The Niagara region is a fertile agricultural area for fruits and vegetables. The best peaches were the ones sold as seconds at roadside stalls because of a wasp sting or other blemish. Sour cherries, sugared and sold in five-gallon pails, made amazing desserts after you had cooked all the jam any family could eat. Good science was applied to agriculture when a local dairy farm started producing grain and vegetables and selling them to passersby, understanding the climate and soil well enough to produce a new variety of sweet corn every two weeks from July to September, winning prizes regularly for field crops at the regional agricultural fair – and shipping frozen cattle embryos to farmers elsewhere who wanted the best dairy herds they could get.

᭥

The food should be different when you travel somewhere else. It should be what the people there have learned to grow and cook as their staple foods, woven together with place, with family and with culture into the foundation of their community life. That is one facet of sustainability.

I recall a story told to me by a friend in India who worked with peasant farmers. A multinational agrichemical company with the best of intentions (and an eye on its profits) decided to develop a strain of potato with extra nutritional value that would grow in the soils of south India. From a technical standpoint, it was brilliant – disease-resistant, drought-resistant, producing vitamins to counter the deficiencies that had long plagued communities in the region and had caused entirely preventable diseases. From a marketing standpoint, it was also brilliant – no doubt funded by those concerned for sustainable development, it promised a yield that would make farmers into perpetual customers of this now patent-protected and very valuable seed.

When I asked what had happened, my friend shrugged and said it was an abject failure, observing dryly, "In that part of India, we don't eat potatoes."

⚜

We need to consider all of the local systems within which the food we eat is woven – social, cultural, economic, political, ecological and technological – or we risk disaster on a global scale never seen before.

The key to food security, to sustainable food for everyone, is to be found close to home, valuing proximity over things at a distance.

I do wonder, though, whether there are also other, more subtle signs that a global diet brings with it problems from a distance. For example, I should mention that we can't cook fish or lobster in our house anymore. For no apparent reason, after years of regular exposure to all kinds of seafood and shellfish, serious allergies suddenly appeared.

The recent and explosive rise in food allergies of all kinds has been noted by people who, like me, grew up on a school lunch diet not of tomato sandwiches but of peanut butter or tuna ones. North American schools today have excluded so many allergenic foods that empty calories and preservatives are the best remaining option for fuelling the school day.

It makes me wonder if these allergies are the result of the constant bombardment of our immune systems, from a young age, by novel proteins and chemicals from environments not our own, to which our bodies are unaccustomed. Perhaps they are triggered by toxins that are never identified in food, rarely tested, from faraway places.

In our case, we were told the allergy must have been triggered by shrimp – obviously not a species native to Manitoba.

Had we stuck to pickerel, I suspect there would have been no problem.

Chapter 2
Knowledge

Years ago, when lobsters barely travelled, my father brought a couple of them home after another business trip to Halifax. My mother was pleased at this treat, but one of her friends, speaking with the relish only ex-Maritimers can bring to the subject of eating fresh lobster, told of a recent dinner party where she had been rebuked by her hostess for displaying similar enthusiasm. Tears in her eyes, the hostess explained that she had cooked lobsters once herself. As long as she lived, she would never forget the sound of their claws on the oven door!

Ecologists are concerned about the rapid decline in biodiversity. We are losing more and more species of plants, animals and other creatures that have survived on Earth for many thousands of years longer than the humans who are causing their extinction.

What is not recognized is that Western culture has done even more damage lately to the store of knowledge accumulated for thousands of years by people within their families and local communities.

We are hemorrhaging useful knowledge at a rate never before imagined. The knowledge, skills and abilities of previous generations are not being passed along to their successors. We stand at the brink of a cultural disaster whose scope and effects are difficult to calculate.

It is all happening right under our noses – not only close to home but within our homes as well.

✺

Knowledge is not the same thing as information. We have lots of information ready to hand (literally) through our cellphones. Individually, we have more accessible information than entire past civilizations, and the amount available continues to grow exponentially.

If information is about "what," then knowledge is a combination of "what" and "how." What information do we have? How should we understand it and use it? In other words, knowledge is information in context.

Even to say this, however, adds a huge assumption to the mix. To define information as "just the facts," outside of any context, is a leap. Apart from automatic sensor readings recorded without comment or sorting in data banks, any information that passes through human hands is within some kind of context. (Even the example of the sensor readings is problematic, because people designed the sensors, the machinery and the computer programs involved.)

Yet we constantly act on the implications of this assumption, talking about collecting and processing data as though it were possible to gain information without interpretation.

Epistemology is one of those nickel-words in philosophy that instantly sparks a huge debate: How do we know what we know? Again, to avoid sliding into the mire, I want to take a pragmatic approach to what happens to knowledge within community.

After all, when it comes to things like understanding climate change, some might dispute the information, but most argue over its interpretation. The rest of us wonder whose version of "the facts" we should believe and whose interpretation of them we should trust.

Looking through the lens of living "close to home" and making better choices today than we did yesterday, the key problem relates to useful knowledge. How does information become knowledge that is useful to us in making decisions, every day? Within what context should we place, understand and then act on the information we receive, at length and in huge volume, every day?

In other words, we are talking about local technology. It is the local technological choices we make ourselves that reflect our values. These technological choices will either mean sustainable development or no sustainable future at all – for any of us.

Technology is not just in our hands. It is in our heads. But technology is also not just in our heads – it is in our hands and, through us, in our communities. Technology drops us, every day, right into the centre of how we interact with each other and with the world around us.

If there are as many kinds of technologies as there are people who choose to do something, in every culture, in every place and all the time – if technology is what makes us human – then what has gone wrong lately in Western culture?

Knowledge is transmitted generation to generation. Depending on the local culture and its circumstances, what continues to be practical is passed along. Strip a contemporary context away from useful knowledge and it reverts to information – quaint and amusing party conversation, but nothing really important. I could build a blacksmithing forge and use it to make simple items – I learned how many years ago, working at a national historic park. In terms of how I live now, it is irrelevant; I get a smile for telling the story, but no one (including my children) is offering to be my apprentice and learn what I know and could teach them.

Returning to the theme of cooking for a less exotic example, there is a technology of food in every family and every community – not just how we grow and harvest it, but how we turn it into something we can eat. Any child old enough to be aware of its surroundings in a Maritime community on the east coast knows lobsters are immersed headfirst in boiling, salted water, or perhaps dropped in a steamer. Either method kills the lobster instantly. Cooking them slowly in an oven would rank right up there with microwaving the cat.

We can write our recipes down in cookbooks, but these recipes – everything from the units of measure to the sorts of special ingredients required – depend on the local circumstances of the person cooking. If the context is vague or the utility of the information is questionable, recipes are just not enough to bridge the generational gap.

Certain cookbooks can take on the aura of sacred scripture for those who swear by their every word. Not knowing the original context, however, can lead subsequent generations to miss rather obvious mistakes.

For example, my edition of the celebrated *Joy of Cooking* instructs would-be lobster eaters to place the lobster in cold, salted water, bringing it slowly to a boil. If there were a Maritimers' version of PETA, it would be picketing the bookstore where such a cruel and inhumane publication was sold!

⁂

The idea of a knowledge economy is utterly deceptive, because it assumes the possibility of "knowledge" without context, able to be transported – or better, transmitted – across distances in time and space, in exchange for something else. While it is possible to transmit information that way, knowledge is only possible in context, and the context of information must be moved as well.

After all, having a conversation with someone about "bits and bites" would have very different outcomes if the context was computer data networks, popular snack food or the perils of putting a bridle on a horse. Information must be framed and interpreted and, at the first level, this requires somebody to do it.

Technological knowledge is always local knowledge. Generating that local context for information requires people.

Sometimes it seems like industrial culture has forgotten this point. It is an obvious extension of the machine analogy, where individuals are regarded as interchangeable parts of the machine. Teachers teach and mechanics fix things – when the skill set for either is dumbed down to a point where teaching is relaying information, and fixing things is replacing one plug-in part with another, then who does it hardly seems to matter.

But systems, even mechanical ones, are rarely (if ever) that simple. The greater the complexity, the more interrelated systems are involved and the more the individual operator's skills and abilities matter.

For example, early technology transfer took place through the migration of people who knew how to do something. When they moved to a new location, they reconstructed the necessary context for communicating their knowledge. Entire industries in the 18th and 19th centuries depended on the attraction and retention of specific individuals from somewhere else – whose personal influence, therefore, was tremendous.

But as knowledge is stripped of context, one of the dimensions stripped away is the personal one – whose idea it was, where it came from, what path they took to making something happen. Using a different word, that context is the story. Any history of the development of Western industrial society that does not include as a central feature the biographies – the stories – of the key people involved is therefore worthless.

When someone eventually writes a history of sustainability, personal stories will be just as necessary to establish and communicate the context of what is going on around us right now.

History is never "just the facts."

�֍

Access to certain kinds of information has never been easier, but knowing what to make of it, or how to choose among competing claims, is increasingly difficult. And knowledge that involves more than verbal description – especially in the use of our bodies, and the experience that increases our skill levels – is at greater risk of simply disappearing.

When we need opinions and advice, we rely on the information found through Google or consult with experts far away because no one close at hand can do what needs to be done. You could call it the "expert fallacy," the presumption that tasks need to be undertaken by someone specialized in that particular kind of work: it means that people consider themselves helpless to solve problems until convinced otherwise. Should the power go out, the natural gas stop flowing, the water dry up or the toilets refuse to flush, too many people have no idea what to do about it.

This is a relatively recent problem, arguably related to a general disintegration (or disappearance) of local communities across the North American landscape – though there is potential of it happening elsewhere, too, as rural populations move into the random anonymity of life in urban shantytowns and slums.

To hearken back to the caricature of pioneer life on the Prairies, settlers needed to be self-sufficient. There were neighbours, though only a few close enough to help in an emergency, and all busy trying to survive themselves. So every family needed to master a certain skill set to live in what were bleak, primitive and (certainly in winter) isolated circumstances.

This meant knowing how to grow foods of all necessary kinds, how to tend the domesticated animals from birthing to tending to slaughter, harness draught animals for plowing, find water and manage it for consumption, build dwellings for people and animals, plant and harvest crops, chop trees and make fires, hunt and trap, fish in all weather, make clothing from scratch, cook and preserve food of all kinds, treat ailments – as long a list as you can imagine life on the Prairies required. (My blacksmithing skills would have been useful, if likely inadequate!)

It didn't mean anyone was good at everything

on the list, or even at most things. Perhaps the skills of a neighbouring family could be exchanged for things you did well. Sometimes there would be a skilled tradesman of some kind who would travel the circuit and tend to one aspect of life, but this would be a rarity in places too far from town.

To put it in a futuristic context, I have always appreciated the way Robert Heinlein's main character summed it up in *Time Enough for Love*: "A human being should be able to change a diaper, plan an invasion, butcher a hog, conn a ship, design a building, write a sonnet, balance accounts, build a wall, set a bone, comfort the dying, take orders, give orders, cooperate, act alone, solve equations, analyze a new problem, pitch manure, program a computer, cook a tasty meal, fight efficiently, die gallantly. Specialization is for insects."

In a couple of generations, we have lost hard-earned skills because they are simply not being passed down to the young people in our midst. In fact, most of the older ones (like me) never learned them in the first place – and our children dismiss these skills, this practical knowledge, as irrelevant to the way they think their lives will unfold.

I have surveyed my classes for years now, asking how many students can do a series of specific things that past generations would have regarded without comment as essential. When I first did this, the positive response rate was about 25 per cent, but it rapidly dropped to 10 per cent, where it has remained till now. Most of those 10 per cent can do most of the things on my list, so it is clearly a more general problem than the loss of one particular skill, such as people not cutting down trees anymore and therefore not needing to learn how to use an axe.

The kind of knowledge passed down through generations of apprenticeship, formal or otherwise, has been largely lost. It was always more than masters and apprentices: fathers taught sons; mothers taught daughters. When your own children refused to learn from you, there were families in the community with whom such instruction could be exchanged. (The butcher's son wanted to be a baker, while the baker's daughter wanted to be a candlestick maker, whose son fortunately wanted to be a butcher!)

Returning to the kitchen, family recipes are just that – to an outsider, it might be just another fruitcake, but to a family member, it was great-great-grandmother Powell's fruitcake, whose secrets have been passed down through the generations on the same tattered recipe card.

We are losing this kind of practical knowledge, to be sure, but it is not too late to recover some of it. I watched my mother cook, bake, pickle and preserve through my childhood – she does a lot of it, still – and have learned how to do some of these things, mostly after I got older and was out on my own; she is still regularly consulted on problems I encounter. But after I surveyed my classes, it bothered me to realize that my own children would fare poorly if asked the same questions.

So, one Christmas when health and weather prevented the usual shopping expeditions, my mother asked what on earth she could buy for a 10-year-old boy. I told her to give him an empty recipe box and offer cooking lessons each time there was an in-service day at his school.

Both players were initially dubious, but from the start it was a hit. Each day he returned with at least one new recipe, some new skills – and something to share with the family for supper. Years later, he is now unafraid of the kitchen, has mastered cooking skills I would attempt gingerly and with less success and has a good relationship with his grandmother.

I wish this were less unusual. In graduate school, I had classmates from all over the world, because this particular university had a generous scholarship for students "from away." As one of few Canadians, I found myself interpreting local mores and cultural practices all the time, so was stunned one day by a confession from the only member of our group who was married back home. His spouse was joining him in March and he confessed to me he had been starving, waiting for her to arrive and cook him a decent meal. He had been living on a steady diet of tomato soup and tuna from a can for eight months, unable to even make a sandwich or a pot of the student staple, macaroni and cheese, because he did not know how.

It was clearly not just an information gap. There were skills involved he needed to learn and to practice, but there was no one to teach him within a cultural context he could accept. These days, you might ask why he did not Google the answer, but that would not have been enough.

Today information from a distance, compiled or authored by strangers considered to be experts, thus tends to be valued and trusted more than knowledge gained from personal experience. This reflects a loss of diversity in response to local conditions and contexts, especially in terms of finding different approaches to solving problems.

After all, there is no pressing need to master a body of information or skills outside of the immediate context of using them – why take the time to commit anything to memory, or to practise the physical skills ahead of time, when what is needed can be reduced to information retrieved from a distance, by cellphone, at the point of use?

While it does not yet exist, "Google Tools" (showing how one holds or swings a hammer, for example) is the likely next step in the internet age. To change the maxim, if the only tool in your Google toolbox is a hammer, it's no surprise that everything looks like a virtual nail!

&

I once had a student who told the class that she had always wanted to plant a vegetable garden but didn't know how. She was at least in her thirties, articulate and intelligent, and this was her wish – someday, she would learn how to plant a garden.

It struck me then that there was something deeper going on here, something behind the loss of knowledge not passed down from generation to generation. I was honoured she felt safe enough to tell us her wish... but it bothered me to hear it.

After all, few things are more elementary than planting a garden. You stick a seed in the ground, water it once in awhile and watch it grow. Little knowledge is involved, and no expertise. If you want to get fancy or keep the family fed through the winter, that requires more planning and skill, but the basics of gardening should be obvious to anyone.

It occurred to me that the problem wasn't just lack of knowledge. It was the inability to learn – to try new things, risk failure, trust your own ability to pick things up as you go, to be willing to make mistakes and learn from them.

Unlike information, knowledge is always local, woven together with where we learn it and where we learn to use it. Yet knowledge does not exist in a vacuum. It requires other people, to teach us, to value what we do, and to join with us in community – in a context where information that has become knowledge can then be turned into wisdom.

Chapter 3
Reality

The image of two people sitting across from each other in a coffee shop, each messaging on a cellphone, is as familiar as it is troubling. The fact that these two people might be grey-haired is a reminder that living close to home has more to do with attitude than geography – and it is not some immature quirk of a younger generation who will eventually grow up and leave such gadgets behind.

We spend more time on reality-at-a-distance than on where we are, whether that means pursuing internet relationships or texting or tweeting instead of hugging friends; spending time on Facebook or Instagram instead of a walk in the park; or online gaming instead of playing football or baseball. Children beginning school might have well-developed thumbs, but they lack the coordination of large muscle groups required to kick a soccer ball; they stand bewildered in clumps on a playground, not knowing how to relate to others in a group activity.

Despite the obvious absurdity, too often we behave as though we live somewhere else, as though our bodies and minds occupy different territory.

If sustainability is about changing behaviour, if the spheres described in this book are ethical spheres that move outward from the choices made by individuals into the larger world, then this disconnection (or dissonance) has to be resolved.

When asked to describe what the world would be like in 2050 – and then what their personal lives would be like by that time – one of my students burst out in frustration, saying she could not reconcile the two pictures. If the world was headed in the direction all the evidence pointed, she could not possibly have the future she envisioned: house in the suburbs, two kids, a dog, vehicles, nice summer vacations, satisfying career and early, comfortable retirement. Somehow we manage to live as though we don't need to reconcile those two scenarios. Something is trumping our instinct for personal and community survival.

Living close to home means living in the here

and now, not some time in the future, not some Other-Where or Other-When. The individual or society that lives for today at the expense of tomorrow has no future; the individual or society that lives for tomorrow at the expense of today will not survive to see it. Somehow, we need a balance between survival today and sustainability for tomorrow, but it has to begin by grappling with the present reality underneath our feet.

We can talk about the ways our communication tools waste our time, but the general fixation with the far away doesn't just apply to electronic communication – the explosive growth in publishing of fantasy books for teens and younger readers, replacing the staples of science fiction, suggests that wallowing in a fantasy world far away that could never exist is preferable to imagining what might be done to improve the real world in which they will possibly live.

Problems in epistemology – to put the more formal label on the concern identified in the last chapter – are thus intertwined with perceptions of reality. We see no value in keeping the practical knowledge of past generations, because we somehow believe that where we live will soon be radically different. The lessons they learned (the hard way) will no longer apply to us or to how we live.

One of the presumptions of Western industrial culture is that we live in a "global village," despite the fact that something like only 3 per cent of the world's population lives outside the country where they were born – and most of them not by choice.

In fact, we don't live in a global village. The global village is illusory at best – and, at worst, is evidence of delusion on a global scale. We live in the village – the community – where our home happens to be. Our relationships, as people, need to be in that community, not some larger, more distant and less material one.

This is a problem in both time and in space. We need to be present where we are, and to value this presence above all other possibilities, if we are to understand the choices we need to make and the reasons why we make them. Otherwise our choices are unsustainable.

As an example of sustainability in practice, the Greek concept at the heart of economics (*oikos*) is hard to match. *Oikos* was grounded in the notion of an estate. Wealth was related to the land a family owned; the land produced agricultural goods that translated into the necessities of life, whether it was food to eat or a surplus to trade.

The responsibility of each generation was to tend the estate, not exploit it, passing it along to the next generation in the same condition – at the very least – as when it was received from the previous generation. Decisions were made for the benefit not only of those enjoying the current harvest but also of future generations who would rely on the estate for their livelihood.

Oikos requires decisions to be made and actions to be taken in the present, not just to preserve the estate but to manage it so that it passes a dynamic system to the next generation. Trees need to be pruned and new ones planted; crops have to be harvested and new ones planted in rotation so the fields are not exhausted; livestock need to be tended and bred to increase the herd; grapes and olives must be picked and processed so that in time the wine and the oil can be used.

A good manager or steward did not allow the concept of "tomorrow" to interfere with what needed to be done today; there was no future excuse for failing to manage the problems and needs of the present.

In our individual and corporate lives, we are far from this ideal; it is frightening to look at how we spend our time and what we focus on instead of managing the needs of the present or of future generations.

❧

A few years ago, just prior to the launch of the video game Halo 3, someone calculated how much time people had spent, worldwide, playing Halo 2. It was estimated to be a billion hours.

Multiply that by the number of potential video game options – more versions of Halo have since been released, for example – and you have some sense of why I would say this: in our harried existence, which apparently leaves no time for a long list of things past generations used to do, it's not about having the time but about how we spend it.

Every recent generation has had its time-wasters – right back to the radio and comic books – but the scale of time spent on unproductive "leisure" activities has increased exponentially with the advent of computer games and now their cellphone variations.

To be clear, all work and no play is never a good idea. Many hours on the prairie farm were spent playing whist, euchre, cribbage and a good number of other games, too. Most, of course, were not solitary – they were group activities, like the board games of yesteryear. These group activities, one might also argue, have merely been replaced by online gaming, with players brought together from around the world to compete against each other over the internet.

Yet I see this as an extension of the psychological distance we have created between where we are and where we live, between the physical coordinates of our bodies and the intellectual coordinates of our minds. Again, there is no harm in escaping the realities of here and now into some fantasy world – I have read fantasy novels since a young age – but there is a problem when people seem to be *living* there.

We will smile at adult fans dressed up as their favourite superheroes at ComiCon gatherings or on Halloween. Yet this kind of activity has become increasingly mainstream, just as the hyper-intensity of the über-fan has made attendance at sporting events increasingly more hazardous. Putting on the "gear" allows the public expression of emotions (and frustrations) that otherwise are locked away inside – an opportunity to let off psychological steam.

Whether by attending football games or going on vacation, people want to "get away" from wherever they are. When that is impossible for physical or financial reasons, temporary escape into the otherworlds provided by our electronic technology will do.

This escape comes at a social cost, of course. Imagine if that billion hours spent playing Halo 2 had been spent picking up garbage or engaging in any kind of socially useful activity – or even just exercising. We would have a cleaner planet and at least some people in considerably better shape!

Beyond the expenditure of time, though, I wonder if the allure of playing Master Chief and battling aliens has something to do with the distortion of reality that distracts us from seeing what is going on right where we live.

❧

Whatever the benefits of electronic communication, from telephone to email to text messaging, from online dating to distance educatión, these technologies must supplement, not replace, the immediate human social interactions we need for our emotional and physical well-being.

While I have no objection to being tagged a Luddite (in my discussion of those mythical figures in *Technology and Sustainability*, I noted that the Luddites were right!), this is not an accurate assessment of my criticism.

Communications technology in the electronic age has reshaped human relationships at a distance. We can now communicate instantaneously, in real time, around the world. I have worked with people I have never met in person, in a variety of countries, and made good friends at a distance whom I hope to meet someday.

As a teacher, I have taught distance courses to students from around the world. We have shared thoughts and feelings, improved skills and grown in understanding just as we would in a physical classroom. I would even argue that participation is actually of higher quality in online discussions because everyone must contribute and there is time and opportunity to do so.

Yet it is simply not the same as being in a classroom together, because the normal communication between people is reduced to lines of type on a screen, telephone conversation or blurry video conferencing. It is only a portion of what could be communicated in person in a course taught by a passionate instructor.

It is no different with long-distance relationships. Internet dating is a booming global business – a far cry from the early days of mail-order brides from catalogues – and it attracts people of all ages.

Older generations will remember courting opportunities at community social events, dances, weddings and strawberry socials, all under the watchful eyes of at least some guardians of public morality, who had to be distracted. In my generation, bars and clubs – cuttingly described as "meat markets" – replaced those kinds of venues. No guardians of morality of any kind were in evidence.

The atmosphere was clearly "let's get physical," to the point that researchers tried to figure out what attracted males and females to each other in such crowded and chaotic environments. They discovered the main attraction for the human animal was smell, isolating chemicals called pheromones that apparently the nose could detect at levels below what instruments could record. You could "smell" your potential mate – and the suitors to avoid at all costs – despite the competing odours in the room.

The next step, of course, was to reproduce and sell these pheromones, packaged in such a way that you could spray on the attractiveness that Nature did not provide. The general idea quickly foundered in a room full of pheromones that made drinking establishments smell like junior high school locker rooms, but there was definitely a smell linked to success.

Fast forward to the internet age. Create a dating profile, invent an avatar, post the best picture of you ever taken (or someone else's picture, for that matter) and go fishing. You are who you want to be, not what (perhaps unfortunately) you are – or smell like.

But at some point the fantasy turns into physical contact – assuming that was the whole point of the internet encounter. I have been told the expression is "going organic" – taking the leap from avatar to in-person meeting, going on a real date in the flesh, not merely a fantasy one in cyberspace.

Imagine your crushing disappointment, however, when the beautiful girl of your dreams, someone who has shared your every joy and sorrow,
turns out to be a 300-pound trucker named Tom –
who is equally disappointed in you.

Reality smells. So do people. No virtual world
can match the physical world – at some point, we
know we are strapped into a machine, that we took
a red pill or a blue one.

Whether we pursue better living through chemicals, alcohol or electronics, at some point we come
down, sober up or power off – and we are back in
our bodies, in our homes, in our communities, in
the reality we tried unsuccessfully to escape.

❧

As I wrote in *Gift Ecology*, we live in a universe of
relations, not an environment of connections. If
there is an emotional barrier to a sustainable future, it is the loneliness people feel – they believe
no one cares for them, so they care little for other
people in return.

This loneliness is the result of retreating into the
global village, leaving behind the village in which
we actually live. When we look for community at a
distance, we will find it – or a semblance of it – in

cyberspace, but it is not the physical community that we need as humans.

This psychological dissonance, between where we live and where we spend our time, contributes to the lack of balance in the choices we make.

So we sit in that coffee shop, texting to others what we are feeling or checking in on friends at a distance instead of focusing on the person in front of us. How many children go untended, put themselves to bed, have no stories read to them or good-night hugs, because their parents are surfing the internet news, finding out what the latest celebrity did or (with greatest irony) posting to Facebook their children's achievements of the day?

Living close to home does not mean ignoring the global village, but it means realizing we don't live there – never did. Nobody real ever will.

Sustainability requires us to start from where we are, to realize the choices we make in the place we live, to engage with the people around us in family and community, and only then move outward in spheres of activity into the larger world.

✄

Interlude

Tipping over the Stool of Sustainability

I am always suspicious of caricatures, even though at times I'm compelled to use them myself. Worse than just using them, however, is claiming that they depict the whole story.

A caricature by a sidewalk artist highlights the subject's recognizable features, but it needs to be appealing enough that someone will pay for it. None of these artists makes a living highlighting the inherent ugliness of their customers. Even satirical cartoonists have to be careful not to cross an invisible line.

The various stock answers to the "what is sustainability?" question are caricatures, meant to appeal to the folks who hopefully will pay the bill that the artist (sustainability consultant) presents. From any other standpoint, however, they are disastrously inadequate, presenting serious obstacles to productive discussions.

Three main caricatures of sustainability make the rounds these days: the Three Pillars of the Stool of Sustainability (Economy, Environment and Society); the pseudo–Venn diagram depicting sustainability as the central overlap of these three elements; and the Three Ps (People, Planet, Profit/ Prosperity), diagrammed however you wish.

The first of these depicts sustainability as the seat of the stool – if one leg is missing, or the legs are not of equal length, the stool doesn't work very well. While I appreciate the fact that equal weight needs to be given to Environment and Society, there are two inherent problems with this caricature:

First, it is static, not dynamic. Using a solid, static object to depict the dynamics of sustainability is fundamentally flawed. Sustainability is simply not a stool.

Second, the caricature only works because Economy is regarded as equal to the other two legs. Requiring them to be of equal length means that economic interests are given equivalency to social and environmental ones (setting aside the issue that everything other than Economy and Environment is morphed into the single leg of "Society"). Quite simply, this is absurd; it means that no effort to fix the leg of Environment or Society can be undertaken if it threatens to harm whatever "Economy" is meant to represent. We may find ourselves in the utterly absurd circumstance of concluding we cannot take the required steps for survival because "we can't afford it."

If I have the only remaining bottle of water (one perhaps that I filled for free) and you need it to survive, you will give me all that you have in order to buy it. To me, it is worth little; to you, it is worth everything you have. The need for personal and social survival thus changes the economic terms of reference. Economy is not a pillar or a goal; it is a means to the end we choose.

The pseudo–Venn diagram suffers from the same basic problem. (I say "pseudo" because a Venn diagram is intended to depict mathematical values; the diagram under discussion here indicates qualitative assessment of concepts or ideas.) Sustainability in this case is the intersection of the three circles or their derivatives. While theoretically it could be argued that the intersection gets larger or smaller depending on the growth or shrinking of the circles, it is a two-dimensional representation of a four-dimensional planetary system. More importantly, it still considers Economy equal in importance to Environment and Society... and allows Economy to operate beyond the point of intersection with the other two components.

If you are just now starting to realize whose interests these caricatures are intended to please, the third one (dating back to the efforts of a multinational oil company to clean up its image in the 1970s) should seal the point. It's not just Economy that is co-equal with Environment and Society this time, but Profits – leaving People and Planet even more vague than their equivalent categories in the other caricatures.

Granted, it has been modified more recently (in some sectors) to "People, Planet and Prosperity" – allowing at least for a feeble rejoinder that survival is a necessary precursor to prosperity – but the same basic problem remains. The diagram varies for this one, but the intention is clear. Perhaps the caricature would be more honest, at least from the perspective of the Occupy or Idle No More movements, if the three Ps were rendered as "Power, Privilege and Politics."

To me, none of these efforts deals with the pressing nature of the specific problems we face. Nor does it offer any real hope in guiding our decisions toward the useful, practical and timely answers – on a global scale – that we need for a sustainable future. We need to go back to the drawing board – or the storyboard.

In searching for a cross-cultural, multifaceted, dynamic and easily understandable representation of sustainability that communicates and manages the complexities of all the systems involved, we need a new story.

Every culture is suffused with stories, but in Western culture we have let some storylines proliferate and dominate without sufficient challenge. The story of things, of stuff, of profits – of a fantasy life in a place far away – has swamped our basic narratives of identity.

We need to live close to home, because that is where these stories are best shared and understood. It is there that the Earth's story can be rediscovered and strengthened, in every place where people look up at the stars and wonder about the meaning of life, the universe and everything.

To lift a reference from the *Hitchhiker's Guide*

to the Galaxy series, the answer is so much more than 42.

PART 2

The Outer Spheres

Chapter 4
Community

The place where I live was once a potato farm, before the farmer, as the saying goes, planted one last
crop of concrete and it was developed into housing
lots. The community is an old one, along the Red
River between Winnipeg and Selkirk, where the
original lots were long and narrow. This gave each
household access to the river, the main transportation route down to Lake Winnipeg (and thence
along river systems to Hudson Bay) or up to the
Forks in Upper Fort Garry (now Winnipeg).

My potato farmer belonged to a later generation
of arrivals, one of the successive waves of Eastern
European immigrants who began a new life on the
Prairies from the late 19th century onward. Their
journey to a foreign country was the result of pov-
erty and strife at home, combined with the promise of 160 acres of land for a $10 registration fee as

long as they improved 40 acres of it and built a home in three years.

Winnipeg was known as the Gateway to the West in those glory years. New communities were planted every so many miles, either as whistle stops or as places to take on water or fuel. There were so many new communities that, to simplify the naming of locations, the railway labelled them along each branch line with names in alphabetical order, from A to Z. Years later, it is possible to map how many communities there must have been simply by noting the missing letters of the alphabet from one surviving town to the next.

There are many stories from those years of hardship and struggle – and of failure. That wave of immigration gave the Canadian Prairies a diverse ethnic identity, rooted in community, that I suspect was unique in the world. People had come "from away," but there was no going back. They made the coldest, most barren spot on the windswept prairie landscape into a place they could call home.

⁂

In older, more established regions, where settlements go back hundreds and even thousands of years, there is not the same understanding of the plasticity of "home." Whether you are a landowner or a tenant, there are still the familiar streets, the familiar buildings and the familiar view of the river, lake or ocean from which one can leave and to which one can always return.

Urban sprawl, redevelopment, population growth and rebuilding from the devastation of war all change the landscape, but I don't think this is the same as walking out on the bald prairie, where no dwelling has ever been constructed as far as the eye can see, and planting a shovel in the sod for the first time. Against all odds, this is my land; against all odds, I will make this my home.

Perhaps this speaks to the tenacity of the descendants of those same settlers who continue to work the land, often taking a job off the farm to cover the shortfalls, working long hours alone, watching their children leave the farm for the city and another life beyond.

It certainly speaks of loss, of the movement from rural to urban areas that has occurred in every country where smallholder farming – the family farm – is to be found. It is also a trend that needs to be reversed to encourage the community well-being at the heart of living close to home.

Those early prairie communities existed to service the farms in the local area. They became the location of grain elevators, country stores, the post office, the church, the school, the police station, the doctor, the dentist, the undertaker – all of the eventual elements of small town life. There, the farm families could socialize, exchange ideas, as well as extra produce, and purchase what supplies they needed to continue to work and live on the farm. The town was the centre, the hub of the wagon wheel, but without spokes and rim, the hub was nothing.

When small farms became larger ones thanks to mechanization, there were fewer people in each area, soon too few to support all those small towns. As the numbers of people shrank, so did the towns, until they became ghost towns along the railway lines, many of which were also abandoned.

This problem continues on the Prairies. The farmers support the remaining towns, to be sure, but it is not so clear that the small towns are supporting the farmers anymore. It is easy to drive a long distance to the city, cheaper to have things ordered online and shipped direct to the farm. There is no longer the same need for (and lack of alternative to) socializing with the handful of people left in the local area.

I was at an agricultural conference about fifteen years ago in southwestern Manitoba to discuss genetically modified crops with farmers. That colleague who worked with peasant farmers in Mumbai had come from India to see Canadian farming first-hand, so he travelled out with us.

We heard at length, both in our billet and in the meetings, about how rural areas were being depopulated, losing their post offices and doctors, and how the farmers were worried that soon their town, too, would become a ghost town.

In response to such heartache, my friend earnestly spoke up, telling the room that in six months he could bring them 500,000 farmers from Mumbai and this would solve all their problems. He was mystified – and a little hurt – when the people roared with laughter, thinking he had told a joke. When the laughter stopped and people realized he was dead serious, there was only a stunned silence.

I was smiling to myself, thinking not only that he was entirely right but that this was precisely how the Prairies were settled a hundred years earlier – just not by farmers from India.

When it comes to rural areas in North America, we have forgotten that smallholder farming was the backbone of the nation until very recently. Industrial-scale agriculture is a recent development, magnified by the Green Revolution into the monster it has become – you can interpret "monster" how you like, whether as a reference to size or to behaviour.

I was once toured around a cattle feedlot in Lethbridge County in southwestern Alberta where the owner apologized for the paltry size of his operation: he was only feeding 10,000 head of cattle, whereas his brother fed 35,000! His silage was packed several stories high by bulldozers on supermarket-parking-lot-sized asphalt pads – but that only lasted until November, so for the rest of the winter, railway grain cars were shunted in to feed the cattle. The wastes were sprayed on the flat landscape, which was watered by irrigation and crossed by only one river – an obvious destination for any runoff from those fields.

I remembered, in contrast, the quaint metal silos that fed my neighbour's 50 head of dairy cattle all winter in southern Ontario, part of that successful mixed farming operation where the manure fertilized the corn and the field crops. I could not help but feel that something had gone terribly wrong.

Some will argue that we have no alternative. More and more people want more and more meat – and they all live in cities. If they want to eat and are willing to pay the price we ask, then full speed ahead.

Instead of the urban areas existing to support the rural areas, the rural areas have become suppliers of whatever the urban areas – especially the cities – demand. If the supply is not available locally, or if the price is too high, the food comes from wherever the price is right. Our cities draw food from the farms in the rest of the world, just as our farms feed cities elsewhere.

The people in those cities who depend on industrial agriculture never see where their food comes from, the conditions under which it is grown or raised or processed. All they see is the shrink-wrapped package on the shelf. If it looks good and the price is as low as can be expected, they will buy it.

Show these city-dwellers even a bit of what

actually goes on in industrial agriculture, especially around meat production, and you will see (as I have) how many are shocked into at least temporary vegetarianism. Yet the one factor that seems to be accepted without challenge is that rural areas, wherever they are found, exist to provide for cities. When food comes from a distance, processed at different points along the way, reciprocity between town and farm simply is not possible, even for the concerned consumer.

We forget that the world has been fed in other ways – and in many places still is. At another conference about food, again with Manitoba farmers, a woman from Bangladesh was a guest speaker. (The gender disparity was evident – the two representatives from the global South were female, but the global North was all male.) She regaled the crowd with her view of Canadian farming from the perspective of an outsider, how thrilled she was to finally be taken out to meet Canadian farmers.

She'd been driven for miles, not seeing anyone except the occasional vehicle travelling in the opposite direction. Finally, arriving at the farm, surrounded by huge machinery, she met "a farmer and his wife." Just the two of them. She asked the room: "What self-respecting woman would want to marry a farmer and move out into the middle of nowhere like that? It must be very difficult for you men to find a wife and keep her."

Then she unpacked her criticisms of industrial farming, how disgraceful it was to leave carrots or potatoes to rot in the field simply because they were not quite the right size. Her community fed everyone in it off a small piece of land, because every inch was used to its maximum, year after year. Nothing went to waste. Ever.

She said how ludicrous it was to plant huge fields of the same kinds of crops, guaranteeing pests – and the need to use chemicals – when, back home, the same crop was planted every seven rows. Mixing things up meant that a pest would starve before reaching the next row it needed to eat.

And weeds? I will never forget her terse observation: "Back home, we don't have any weeds. We only have plants for which we have not yet found a use."

It was delightful – not just because of the humour in her presentation – but as a reminder of the ways in which our recent elaborations of rural and urban life, from country fields to urban plates, are the product of choices that were unnecessary as well as unsustainable.

⁂

Yet, on the other side of the fence, mega-cities are with us to stay, growing in population as well as density, sprawling out into the countryside and replacing fertile agricultural land with "development." In the split between country and city, the snob factor has definitely been on the urban side, until now.

City slickers and country bumpkins have deep roots as characters in the narrative tradition, especially in North America. But in terms of community spirit and those survival skills I listed earlier, the edge definitely goes to the country folk these days.

When we consider the implications of climate change, especially relating to extreme weather, terms like "adaptive governance" and "community resilience" are murmured. How will urban areas cope with the inevitable shocks that accompany global warming? What happens when the lights go out, when the water rises or the drought never ends? If the trucks stop running, how will the city slickers feed themselves? What can be done to promote resilience, enable adaptive responses to climate change, maintain community well-being despite ongoing difficulties or, suddenly, in the face of disaster?

And how can you call it a "community" when people don't know their neighbours anymore or when the "city" is larger in population than entire countries that have seats in the United Nations?

Cities, especially mega-cities, will be the agents of change or of devastation in the near term. They emit huge amounts of greenhouse gases, are major sources of industrial pollution into the air and water, generate millions of tons per year of wastes of all sorts and have a massive ecological footprint. But they also have the potential to reverse their travel along each of these pathways to planetary degradation. Local governments that actually address their own circumstances can have a significant effect on the global mitigation of climate change – because of population density, lifestyle changes in cities affect more people more rapidly. Cities can be crucial in reducing consumption and developing sustainably.

What if cities became laboratories for lifestyle change? If local governments determined the parameters of well-being for the people who live in the community – and then acted on those parameters – change would happen much more rapidly than if the same decisions were made by governments at a distance. It means owning the choices locally, recognizing what is involved, what the benefits will be – and then choosing to accept the costs.

Yet cities also have the potential to be much more than mitigators. Waste reduction and pollution control, however critical, are not enough to drive lifestyle change, certainly not to the extent that a global transformation requires. Cities need their own story, one that describes a place where the community is vibrant, life is enjoyable and the future is a place of possibility, not merely grim survival. Peer pressure works best when you are surrounded by a lot of peers; the daily support of friends and family is most effective when you see them every day.

Vibrant cities have distinct neighbourhoods where everybody actually does know your name. Urban anonymity leads to social decay, psychological distress and a general overall decline in personal and community well-being.

Living close to home means knowing who lives next door and down the street. It means being able to shop and access services locally. It means knowing and working with local people to manage local problems. It means building relationships with each other in ways that increase resilience to the inevitable stresses and shocks that life always brings to any community. It means wanting to volunteer, not just being asked or coerced into it.

To move away from a purely economic model of assessing quality of life, we need to move toward another one. There are community indicators, data that can be collected and compared across regions of a city, correlating the stuff of daily life with outcomes relating to well-being. One such project in Winnipeg posts data on a website from a variety of sources but goes beyond numerical aggregates to interpret what life is like for residents by having them tell their own stories in short videos. It recognizes, by doing this, that life itself is a "cross-cutting issue."

Behind every face there is a story; well-being requires some kind of communal "fire" around which people can both hear the stories of others and tell their own, an opportunity to relate to other people outside of the roles and tasks that otherwise fill our lives.

⚜

Chapter 5
Economy

In some ways, we could blame the unsustainable global society on the success of Henry Ford – specifically, on his Model T.

I don't mean the successful mass production of a car that was launched in 1908 and concluded its run in 1927, or the fact that the Model T (more than any other automobile except perhaps the Volkswagen Beetle) defined what car ownership meant to so many people. Nor do I blame its design persistence, with so many of its features still to be found in automobiles today, which demonstrates the ingenuity and system vision of its designers.

From a sustainability perspective, many of those features are admirable: finding a design that worked and keeping it for nearly two decades; telling consumers they could have any colour they wanted, as long as it was black; selling a vehicle that could be turned into anything that was needed to supply power, and so on.

It was the same with the Ford Motor Company: reducing work hours to eight; paying the highest wage in the industry; perfecting the production assembly line; dropping the price of the vehicle so Ford workers could buy their own product. These were admirable corporate traits that would be applauded today.

The biggest problem was that Henry Ford only accepted cash. It was a moral position, imposed on would-be car owners much like the colour of car that they could buy. It was good business sense, ensuring people worked for what they had. It was part of his personal moral philosophy, which also led him to ensure that his workers and their families were good representatives of Ford in the community by having his own social welfare squads check up on how things were going at home.

It was such an overwhelming success that competitors had to find another way into the market or just give up, as so many did in the early years of automobile manufacture. Don't like black? We will sell you another colour. Don't like being told how to live? We only want you for your work – what you do the rest of the time is up to you. Don't have the money right now? We will give you credit.

In the midst of the unfolding global economic crisis, to say that "credit" has a lot to do with our problems is an obvious point. At the heart of our economic system is a fascination with money-at-a-distance in an artificial economy that leaves individuals vulnerable to "market forces" outside their control.

From the moment the General Motors Acceptance Corporation was formed in 1919 as a way of undermining Henry Ford's cash-only stranglehold on the automobile industry, credit, investment and interest have evolved into a system that defers returns and payments, selling dreams and too often returning nightmares for the small investor. The concepts of credit and investment shift the economy away from the here-and-now and create relationships to a future that may never exist.

Credit has become a way of life. You either have it or you don't. It determines our options for everything from buying a car to attaining housing to starting or expanding a business. Yet what is credit? It is a present offer of money for a future return of that money plus more for the privilege.

In effect, it is long-distance cash – long-distance in time – and its vulnerability is little different than those other products we receive from a distance in space.

The longer the time frame, the riskier it is for both the lender and the borrower. One could argue that the ongoing global financial crisis is a product of the final recipient being removed further and further from the initial reason for the borrowing, as with the high-risk subprime mortgages. When the "fundamentals" are so future-oriented, supposed loan security is little more than the proverbial skyhook.

As for investments, we make them thinking we know the economic future, but we don't – and the result is therefore speculative. If we are right more often than we are wrong, then we make money, but this depends less on our own prescience or ability than on unpredictable intangibles.

One wonders if this is anything more than an elaborate pyramid scheme in which new investors are attracted by a promise of future returns over which there is no control, while the new investments provide a return to those whose money is already invested. The pyramid collapses, of course, when the potential investor realizes that there will be no return like the one promised and so refuses to participate; this is called "a crisis in investor confidence."

After all, the promise of future return on investment is based on the expectation of something for nothing. Present expectations are deferred in the hope of satisfying more of them down the road. The slightest doubt that such a future return will happen then leads to investors clawing back whatever they can, preferring a substantial loss to the obliteration of their investment.

Even the glimmer of a potential loss will drive seniors to cash in the retirement investments on which their income depends. The sight of those retired or nearly retired having their lives shaken or destroyed by stock market fluctuations is a sobering disincentive to the younger members of society encouraged to "invest for retirement" in the variety of stock market vehicles available.

Paying off debts, buying land, investing in gold bars – or simply putting money under the mattress – all seem like wiser options than the "something for nothing" promise of stock market investment. Should pension plans decide that there are less risky options for the investment of their members than mutual funds, moreover, there will be serious consequences for the availability of investment capital for business. Something for nothing always risks becoming nothing for something.

The greater the distance between initial loan and eventual investor, the less certainty there is of the future return on the investment and thus the more vulnerable the system becomes to both speculation and loss of confidence. The fatal flaw in risk management of such a long-distance financial system is the lack of any buffer against the eventuality that the whole system itself is flawed. This goes beyond the need to protect against an occasional economic meteor strike and its effects; there is no safeguard against the more serious consequences of unchallenged axioms about the global economy and their unsustainable implications.

The neighbour who loans a hay baler to another farmer has a strong likelihood of having the baler returned, with the agreed number of extra hay bales as compensation. The fact that they are neighbours and that there will be future interaction, as well as the relationship between the loan and the return on investment, anchors the transaction in the real and the local. The loan is made out of surplus – he didn't need the baler at the time – and the return is minimal enough that the borrower can afford to complete the transaction out of his own surplus of hay bales.

We could digress into a discussion of reals versus unreals here, the difference between pork bellies in the future and actual pigs here and now. But whether those pork bellies are distant in time or in space – or worse, both! – from the investor, the problem is primarily that of distance.

The medium of exchange also entails distance in time as well as space. Not only is the medium immaterial – physical cash rarely changes hands – but transactions often involve loans, which are payment at some future time and not at the point of the transaction. Thus money that is not local is as vulnerable as any other commodity; localization of money depends on being able to see where our money is and being assured that it will return to us as expected and in the right amount.

Unreals can have real consequences, but only because of a misplaced focus on something distant, as opposed to something close at hand. When we focus on reals, on things we can kick, there is a local reality on which to fall back.

The creation of a globalized industrial market, with capital easily transported from country to country, region to region, focuses local industries on investor satisfaction instead of job satisfaction, keeping the distant owners of capital happy rather than the workers in the community. One-industry communities, where the majority of the jobs are related to a single commodity, are increasingly vulnerable to external forces outside their control. The less local control there is over employment in the community, the less resilience there is when conditions "away" change, making the community itself less sustainable.

This is another way of characterizing the shift in the dominant economic structures of Western culture that dates back to the Age of Discovery and then the series of industrial revolutions.

Historically, agrarian societies fed themselves first, and relied on surplus food supplies as a source of trade with other societies. The same pattern applied to communities within the society and families within the community – one group would barter its extra produce for another's. Trade depended upon surplus. If there was no surplus, there was no trade, but there would still be the basic necessities for survival until the next year. When production fell beneath subsistence, people either died or migrated.

The First Industrial Revolution, circa 1750, is credited or blamed with instituting huge social changes, but the pattern of trading production surplus to local needs remained intact in the agricultural sector until very recently. Even in postwar societies, a large percentage of the population either lived on the farm or derived income from the farm, and sufficient local production of the main necessity, food, was a focus of the family and the community. Recipes, like techniques of planting and preserving fruits and vegetables, were recorded and passed down from generation to generation, as were the necessary skills in everything from handcrafts to handyman tasks, creating a local, stable economy in which local knowledge was preserved and developed.

A preference for the local was inescapable – for one thing, that was all most people saw of the world. Even as tourism began to grow – the consequence of surplus money – most people did not venture far from where they lived, and if they did, they carried home with them in a camping trailer.

Industrial culture has replaced such a reliance on local organic systems with dependence on mechanical systems, fostering dependency on distant producers (of raw materials) and consumers (of manufactured goods). Trade results from surplus money – but too often it is an artificial surplus derived from credit, not from production surplus to local needs. The greater the dependency on those distant (and often invisible) players, the more vulnerable will be the local industries on which people's livelihoods depend.

Quite simply, this complex system is inevitably vulnerable to any number of disruptions, intentional or natural, compounded with the equally inevitable tendency to shift environmental or human costs of production elsewhere from the point of consumption.

It also increases the scarcity of irreplaceable local resources. The water that goes into crops is shipped outside the watershed and arguably disrupts the local hydrogeological cycle, especially in a time of water scarcity. Industrial pollution ruins local habitat at the point of production, not the point of consumption, so beyond the water used to make things is the problem of contaminating remaining local sources.

We don't account for these externalities as we should, because there is no acceptable balance-sheet approach to deciding what they are worth that includes qualitative as well as quantitative assessments. How do you calculate "well-being" – and who should do the math?

While much more could be said on this point, here I would simply contrast this situation with sustainable economics, if we can apply such a label to economies that focus on local essentials and trade only that which is actually surplus. Certainly there has been a serious effort made to find ways of anchoring a local economy, including local currency, to create production and consumption systems that are less complex and more local. Security for both credit and debt is located in the community and its relationships.

Trade balances between imports and exports need to be rethought from the perspective of quality of life at both ends. After all, should we consider local community "well-being" a commodity able to be traded and sold?

A sustainable local economy is one that enables the local community to be sustainable in all of its aspects in the long run. If the local economy is not sustainable, its future has been traded away – literally – to people at a distance, for the proverbial bowl of stew.

Chapter 6
Ecology

When the road is not covered with ice and snow, I enjoy taking early morning walks down to the river. Away from the distractions of the rest of the day, it is a chance to think and to appreciate more of my surroundings than a busy life permits.

My small yard is always full of drama and surprises. The little woodlot (of scrub oaks) is overgrown – but this summer, those scruffy bushes at the edge turned out to be high-bush cranberries that produced a bushel of fruit. Last year, we found wild plums, prairie roses, wildflowers – all mixed in with hardy Scotch thistles.

There are birds flying everywhere, squirrels a chattering nuisance, rabbits grazing, hawks dropping in for dinner, crows pecking at whatever. In the winter, birdseed needs to be scattered around the yard in enough locations so all the various creatures – only some with wings – don't fight too much over the food.

When the season changes and the geese announce their return, I am deafened by the sound of frogs in the ditches after a good spring rain. But after I cross the highway and walk down toward the river, I am struck by the silence. Golf-green grass, neat yards, shaved ditches, pruned trees – and silence. No frogs, so sounds, not even birds, except those flying through.

Just silence. It is an uneasy feeling, like walking through a fantasy wood where something is seriously wrong, an absence of normal life, until I reach the river's edge.

We have taken a wandering path to the obvious point of what "live close to home" must mean. Home is where we plant our feet, lay our heads at night, cook and eat our meals, where family is rooted and community begins.

But as on my early morning walk, when we take the time to observe exactly where we live, there will be surprises – many of which will not be good. Should we be able to explore the air, the water and soil; the roots of trees and plants; the lives of the animals that live where we do; there will be evidence of sickness, an unravelling of the web of life.

No part of the planet is unaffected by the consequences of human activity, nor is any plant or creature left untouched. You could say that today all ecology has become social ecology, because we can no longer isolate ecological systems and observe how they function independent of influence by society and culture.

※

Climate change affects us all. We are at the mercy of weather systems and climatic problems that start far away, over which we have no control. Because of that distance, we don't feel any urgency to change how we live, because it seems such local changes will have little or no effect on the bigger picture.

Yet it all depends on how you understand planetary climate patterns. We focus on those macro-climatic conditions, the large things like hurricanes and widespread drought, rising sea levels and warming oceans. All of these are compilations (which admittedly take on a dynamic of their own) of micro-climatic conditions, things that happen very close to home, over which we do have influence and even some control.

Choose to cut down all the trees on the mountainside and watch erosion, floods and mudslides change the local ecology beyond recovery. Dam up a river and prevent it from reaching the sea and watch everything change in the whole watershed, from precipitation to growth of new species in stagnant water to changes in the coastal waters where the rivers used to flow.

Deserts will expand, foot by foot – but they can be reclaimed the same way through careful cultivation and water retention strategies. Trees can be replanted, water courses allowed to flow once again through to the sea – Nature has an astonishing resilience and regenerative capacity, but it happens in one small area at a time.

⚜

Working from the local to the global, we need to make choices that are sustainable in our local environment, where we have control over the quality of the air, water and soil, over how we treat the plants and animals that share our living space. Environmental problems started small and grew over the last 150 years; these problems can be reversed in the same way, though it will likely take just as long to undo the damage.

The importance of the near at hand to a sustainable future should be obvious. The air we breathe, the water we drink, the soil we walk on – like the food we eat – is as local as it gets. Yet the devaluing of proximity takes its toll on this aspect of our lives, as well.

If we engage in ecologically destructive behaviour, it is on such a small scale that we think it doesn't matter very much. If we make the sacrifices we should to reduce our ecological footprint, this is an equally small solution on a planet where many others continue to make destructive choices.

In both cases, paralysis results. If we were to value proximity in ecology as we should, we would make sustainable choices in our local environment and change how we treat the plants and creatures that share our living space.

For example, in light of the decades-old environmental-movement mantra that "there is no such place as 'away,'" keeping the waste we generate locally would mean being confronted every day with the environmental consequences of our personal consumption – something that would definitely motivate more sustainable choices!

The only way to drive home the environmental

effects of industrial and other human activities is to replace the NIMBY syndrome (Not in My Back Yard) with JIMBY (Just in My Back Yard). If we were not allowed to throw things "away" or to bring things home from "away," the necessary life-style changes would be obvious.

Environmentalists lament the decline in biodiversity, for we are losing more and more species of plants, animals and other creatures every year, species that have survived on Earth for many thousands of years longer than the industrial culture that is pushing them over the edge. Attempts to conserve biodiversity, protect endangered species and preserve habitat exemplify the application of the "live close to home" principle to environmental issues.

❧

An increased focus on local ecosystems would compel us to understand our surroundings in terms of watersheds.

Without clean water, everything dies. In a warming world, places already dry will likely become drier. Extended periods of drought are projected in regions that, until now, have supported industrial-scale agriculture. Aquifers in these same regions are seriously depleted. Large cities around the world are pumping away the ground under their feet, sinking significantly below sea level.

We must stop defining our international relationships entirely by lines drawn on a map by humans; instead, we must honour those etched into the surface of the Earth by running water. Ecological topography should become more important than political geography, because where the water flows affects all living things along its path.

In places where water is already a precious and scarce resource, conflicts have occurred for other reasons. Adding a fight over water to an already explosive situation can't lead anywhere good.

Climate change could easily lead to "climate wars," not over territory for access to trade routes or traditional resources but over clean water, water for irrigation, water for industry, water for clean power generation. Given the weapons available and the desperation of people deprived of life's necessities, such local wars could be catastrophic for the planet as a whole.

This is one of the reasons why "economy" has to be understood as a tool, not as a goal in itself.

The goal must be sustainable local communities, each contributing to sustainable regions in the same watersheds, whatever the political lines on a map might once have been. Lack of a shared understanding, lack of collective wisdom – these can only have disastrous consequences.

In a round world, there are no corners in which to hide or take shelter.

⁂

It would be nice to think that the momentum of an unsustainable lifestyle is the accidental product of history and circumstance, that when people realize what they are doing, they will obviously change their values and behaviour.

Some have, others will – but not all. There is much ado about "green" these days – green business, green transportation, green industry, green economy; not to mention green products, green lifestyle and green whatever-can-be-painted-that-colour.

This emphasis generates a backlash, in some cases, no doubt, from fair-minded people who are not willing to be greenwashed into paying for a future they don't think is likely or necessary. They can be persuaded to change by showing them whatever evidence is required. But the greening of everything also generates hostility from those whose lifestyles and attitudes are unlikely to change, regardless of what they are told or shown.

Some may think they are insulated by privilege, power or geography from the effects of climate change or environmental degradation; changing circumstances will certainly break down that attitude in time. But there are still others whose values and choices are simply anti-Earth and need to be labelled that way.

We now diagnose someone who demonstrates a lack of moral responsibility or social conscience, perhaps with a propensity toward violence against other people, as having antisocial personality disorder (replacing the combination of the terms *sociopath* and *psychopath*, each with a checkered history of diagnosis and demonstration). I suggest we need a similar diagnosis of people who demonstrate a lack of moral responsibility or social conscience toward the Earth and to future generations.

These people are unconcerned by their ecologically destructive lifestyles, by business activities that focus on profit for themselves without regard to human or environmental costs and by their support of weakening environmental policies that ensure further devastation. By their anti-ecological behaviour, they demonstrate a propensity to damage the places where others live, both now and into the future.

While it might take a while for the *Diagnostic and Statistical Manual of Mental Disorders* to include this diagnosis and give it a name – like anti-ecological personality disorder – for now it will serve to label such people as "terrapaths."

Perhaps when we can finally shed the label *green* and replace it with *smart* or *wise*, we will encounter less opposition to the lifestyle changes we must all make – except from those who, by virtue of a psychological disability, will continue their unreasonable and morally irresponsible course toward planetary disaster.

Recent history is full of examples of what happens when leaders of countries are psychologically incapable of making wise decisions for their own people or for others because of their antisocial personality disorder. We need to add the ecological equivalent to this cautionary list and also ensure that terrapaths at any level are not allowed to determine our collective future.

Gift Ecology described the "mechanical model" that has come to dominate Western thinking since the time of the Renaissance – everything is a mechanism, including the world around us. Linearity, predictability, method and perpetual growth have been part of that model, which has grown in power and strength over the past five centuries. This is the foundation of the modern society in which we live, but it has also guaranteed the problems that our generation must solve.

Many people have criticized this model over the years. One alternative maintains that we must understand the world around us as a kind of steady state system, one in which there is balance and reciprocity, where new life and growth is possible only as death and disintegration occurs.

Where the mechanical model derives from a machine, the steady state model reflects the dynamic balance of life within a contained ecosystem. While the latter is obviously preferable as a reflection of living systems rather than mechanical ones, it is also inadequate for understanding ecology in a climate-changing world.

We no longer live in a time of equilibrium, of

balance, where decisions made today may be based on what worked before. Predictability has become impossible because it depends on an understanding of all the components of the system. We no longer understand even as much of the global system as we thought we did 50 years ago. In our current situation, the steady state model is just as inadequate and ineffectual – even as dangerous – as the mechanical model.

Instead, we need a dynamic model, one that is adaptive, mitigative and regenerative – one in which the players adapt to changing local conditions as necessary and try to mitigate the causes of further changes – that relies upon and enhances the natural capacity of Earth to regenerate, to "upcycle" and to flourish right where we live. As William McDonough and Michael Braungart state in their book *The Upcycle*, "the goal of the upcycle is a delightfully diverse, safe, healthy and just world with clean air, water, soil and power – economically, equitably, ecologically, and elegantly enjoyed."

Understanding our dilemma in terms of this kind of dream, rather than framing it as an ongoing nightmare, encourages and enables people to do something. Such a dream is powered by hope and strengthened by community.

There is, of course, only one place where that dream can take root and grow into a sustainable future. The further we stray from that place – in mind, in spirit or in body – the more such a dream will fade.

We need to live close to the source of our strength, the source of our hope, the source of our power.

We need to live close to home.

Postlude
Live Close to Home

As individuals, as a culture and as a society, we have increasingly emphasized the metaphorical global village over the village in which we actually live. Whatever the arguments in support of globalization, our preference for the far away at the expense of what is close to home is at the heart of the environmental and social catastrophes that we will soon be forced to confront, wherever we live and whatever our personal circumstances.

Life is not lived at a distance; it is lived in physical and chronological space, here and now. To know people a world away but not the ones next door, to have wonderful relationships with people known only through a computer screen, is to ignore the real world in which we actually live.

Life smells; everything is supposed to smell, especially people, and while virtual reality may sometime in the future create smells to go along with sights and sounds, or food processing corporations may fabricate smells as they now mimic flavors, an odourless world is a poor substitute for the one it attempts to replace.

As we relate to where we actually live, the people around us, our local community and the needs and opportunities it presents, we are able to extend that awareness to the local lives of people in other places.

This awareness, that we all need to live close to home, should be at the heart of globalization, what it means to be a "global citizen." Person to person, community to community, enabling local sustainability in all of its dimensions through relationships is the only practical counter to the negative effects of trying to live at a distance. Applying the concept of *oikos*, we need to recognize the resiliency of all the global systems of our planet – environmental, social and economic – when they are based on strong local systems over which we have control.

If we live close to home, if we focus on changing and improving those local aspects of our lives that we can, the system effects of such a transformation can only be positive.

I live on Treaty 1 land in Manitoba. Here, in the west of Canada, the British government dealt with First Nations people and signed treaties unlike those found elsewhere in the world between the people "from away" and those whose land they wanted to settle.

What this means still is being negotiated in ways that respect Aboriginal tradition, but respect for each other and for the land is always a good place to start any discussion.

Unlike the experience of my great-great-grandmother's generation, whose land in the east was simply taken and their stories, like their families, assimilated or forgotten, here on Treaty 1 land, the stories of Turtle Island are honoured.

So my walk down to the river has another context, one of a relation to the Earth that goes beyond the laws and practices of the people "from away" who planted their crops and built a home here.

Ecologian Thomas Berry's "dream of the Earth" requires that understanding of relations between people and the rest of the Earth. It is a dream, to be sure – one of wholeness and peace along a path of enlightenment that seems very far from how we are living today. It seems so far away, in fact, that it would be easy to dismiss his dream as fantasy, but it is not. There is, after all, a big difference between the two.

We use fantasy to escape from reality, only to eventually (and reluctantly) return to the way things are, unchanged. But a dream is a story that guides our way forward. We dream from where we are. While we work for and walk toward whatever future that dream holds, we accept that we may never see it ourselves – but that doesn't change what we choose to do now.

As part of that dream, we need to reinvent what it means to be human. In Berry's words, this is our "great work," what our generation has been called to do on the Earth.

While his words are inspiring, I prefer to see our task as a rediscovery of something that communities around the world, in small places, have never forgotten. They are the reservoir of our resilience, if we have the wisdom to accept what the elders have to teach us. In those small places, in the heart of true community, lies the true power of what it means to live close to home: the power to regenerate, for new life to emerge full of possibilities we could never predict.

And so we need stories. Stories not only create community – they transform it. According to Thomas King, "the truth about stories is that's all we have." Hearing a story even once changes who we are, forever.

As the landscape is torn apart, the Earth is destoried, because the stories of the people were always tied to the world that they knew, the land they had walked, the waters from which they drank. Air, trees, animals all came to life in the stories because that was how they were experienced every day.

Our modern stories are rooted in events, usually events caused by people; even if Nature starts a story, it is finished by how people respond. These narratives focus on the "I," not the Earth. We leave a fractured and unravelled world view to subsequent generations, instead of one with a weave strong enough to withstand the changes that are coming in the water, in the soil and in the winds that blow across a warming and melting world.

In the Dreamtime of our generation, we need

to walk the storylines that are everywhere, because that is the only way we will find our way back home.

❧

I have spoken often in these books about stories, about the need to gather around the cultural fires of our generation and find again the meaning of Earth, the importance of community and the value of finding, wherever we are, a place to call home.

There is a difference between moral stories and parables, however. Moral stories have the characters and plot worked out – the moral is clear to whoever hears the story. Parables raise questions rather than giving answers; they are not as easily understood, because the players and the plot are more ambiguous.

And so it seems right, in closing, to complete the circle that began with *Gift Ecology* by telling you a parable of Earth:

There was a time when giants walked the Earth. Nothing was safe from what they did. The air turned brown and yellow, choking every breath. The water became poison to drink, flowing black in one place and growing green and foul in another.

The night was shattered by harsh light and the day turned black by smoke as the Earth burned.

It seemed the Earth was at war with itself. Armies of giants laid waste about them wherever they fought. Sometimes, in the battles between giants, one would die. Where it died, everything was robbed of life, as the water became poison, the soil blackened and life was sucked out of the air and all the creatures that lived there.

As the war between giants went on, there were more and more of these dark places. Death seemed inevitable. As the shadow grew, so did fear and then despair.

There were a few places of green and light, places of sanctuary where trees still grew, where the soil brought forth plants to take in the sunshine that came through the smoke, where the air was a little cleaner, the water in its pools a place where the odd fish could survive. The few animals that found refuge by chance never left, because here at least they could be safe for the moment.

In one of these sanctuaries, in a grove with a few small surviving oak trees, lived a family of squirrels. Many dead trees stood in the woods around them, but there were acorns around when the weather turned colder. Dug into the peat soil close to the trees, where earthworms still churned, were also the acorns buried by ancestors long gone.

A small pond, sheltered from the sun by an outcrop of rock and fed by an underground spring that was still clean, gave water enough. By some miracle, small fish lived in it, cleaning the bottom, while two small frogs ate the mosquito larvae that somehow still survived to hatch on top of the water.

In this grove there also lived a family of field mice and some voles whose eyesight never led them more than a few feet from their home. Birds would land in the trees, appreciating the refuge, but soon flew away to look for somewhere better to live.

A rabbit, old and gaunt, found the pool by accident one day. The other animals cared for him, healed what ailments of his they could and listened to the stories he told in return. They learned about the war, the giants, all the terrible things that were going on outside the little sanctuary they called home.

One day, the angry sounds of war seemed very close. The animals cowered in silence, afraid of what might come next without knowing what it would be.

Suddenly, something large crashed through the dead trees, thrashing: a giant. He fell behind the rock outcropping, landing next to the pool with a thud that shook acorns from the trees.

He was silent, his eyes closed. There were terrible gashes in his body, blood dripping off cuts on his face.

"Is he dead?" chittered one baby squirrel.

"I don't think so," said the mother.

The rabbit hopped closer to look. "No, he is still alive. But I fear not for long. Somehow, we must get him away from the pond and the trees, or when he dies, we will all die, too."

The other animals gasped in fear. A field mouse squeaked, "Run away!"

But that was not an answer for the fish, for the frogs, for the earthworms chewing through the soil under the oak trees – they couldn't run away. Besides, where would any of them go? This was their home.

The rabbit sat back on his hind legs and frowned. "We can't move him. He is too large. The only way he will move is if we can heal him enough to move himself."

"Then so we shall," said the mother squirrel.

"We may fail, but it is the only thing we can do to save ourselves and our home." And so the animals scurried around, baby squirrels bringing water to his lips in tiny acorn caps. The rags he wore were stripped away with sharp little teeth, his new wounds licked clean and staunched with peat moss dug from under the oak trees, while maggots were clawed from the dirt and carefully placed in the old wounds to eat away the dead flesh. The animals dug up roots and pushed them into his mouth, hoping he would chew and eat them.

And they waited. Darkness fell and the sounds of war drifted away, leaving an eerie silence.

Still they waited. As morning came, the sun breaking through in places where the smoke was thinnest, the giant stirred, opening his eyes.

He groaned. Startled by the roots in his mouth, he spat them out, but he only managed to pull himself up with one arm to sit, leaning hard against the rock by the pool.

As he focused his eyes in the dawn light, he saw the animals, sitting and watching him. The fish idled at the top of the water; the frogs stared.

The giant had never seen anything like this before. He did not know what it meant.

The old rabbit spoke: "Giant, you have been hurt badly. We have tried our best to heal you, but please leave this place. We are afraid you will die here, and we will all die with you."

The giant swallowed with amazement. He had never seen animals this small before, or lain on the ground where there were flowers, green grass, even a butterfly landing nearby. But he could not speak, so he shook his head.

The old rabbit's shoulders sagged and he turned away. "It's no use," he said.

There was a fearful commotion among the other animals. The field mice ran around in circles, the baby squirrels leaped from branch to branch, chittering. Even the voles came out from under cover and ran aimlessly through the grass by the pond.

The mother squirrel commanded them all to stop this commotion and keep trying to heal the giant. And so they did.

Days passed, but still the giant grew weaker. He needed more to eat than the roots they would bring to his mouth.

The old rabbit watched all of this unfold, knowing that their efforts were fruitless but unable to look away. This was how the community had treated him, he thought, when he staggered into the thicket and found the pond that day.

There was something only he could do. He went to the mother squirrel and said simply: "It is my turn to help. There is one thing I can do that none of you can do, one thing to give back a chance of life to the community that gave me a home."

He looked around at the puzzled faces of his friends and then slowly hopped onto the giant's body, moving up to where he could look into the giant's eyes.

"Help them," he said. "Save their home."

Then the old rabbit took one last breath and died. Everyone looked away as the giant carefully ate the rabbit and then went to sleep.

When the sun came up the next morning, there was quiet in the sanctuary. The giant's skin was a better colour, and he was more alert as his eyes took in the activity starting again around him.

The mother squirrel came up to him and said: "Please try and leave now. We have given everything we can give you, done everything we can, to heal your wounds. Please go."

For once, the giant was able to speak and respond. He said: "Good mother, I cannot move. My back was hurt and my legs will never work again. I can lift one arm, but it is not enough to move me. I am so sorry."

Had the rabbit been listening, he would have been amazed. Giants did not speak to animals and never, ever did they apologize about anything. In fact, this was why they fought all the time – none of them would ever say he was sorry.

"So you will die here, then?" the mother squirrel asked.

"Yes," said the giant.

The animals gasped in fear, but the mother squirrel rose up on her hind legs and scolded them all: "He found this place by accident, just as we all did. We have made it our home and it will be his home until he dies, too. We will care for him as we would care for each other."

And so they did.

The giant grew weaker and weaker until he knew it was the end. The animals gathered around him one last time, knowing that it was the end of everything for them, too. The baby squirrels cuddled up against their mother. And they all waited.

The giant looked out at the scene around him and, for the first time in his life, knew he had found a home and a family. He knew, too, what would happen to them when he died.

And so he started to cry. Giants never cry, but he did. Large teardrops rolled down his face, dripping off into the ground around him as the animals watched with tears in their own eyes.

"Goodbye, my friends. I am so sorry," the giant said. Then he died.

But as the giant died, the miracle happened. Everywhere the tears found the ground, there was a green spark of life. Instead of the ground turning black and the water being poisoned, it was like a thousand springtimes rolled into one in the soil where his body lay.

The darkness did not spread that day the giant died. It was pushed back.

That green patch grew and grew. Nothing could slow its growth. It was so powerful that many of the giants fled in fear. Some did not run away but sat quietly as it spread over them and they, too, became a part of the Earth reclaiming itself.

They had learned what it meant to finally find a Home.

One Earth. All we have. All there is.
Miigwech.

Bookshelf

As this is the third book in the series, the bookshelf sections of *Gift Ecology* and *Technology and Sustainability* include much of the same material that influenced *Live Close to Home*.

I would add to this list some recent publications, such as John S. Allen's *Home: How Habitat Made Us Human* (New York: Basic Books, 2015), which I discovered only after my manuscript was virtually complete. It is a useful and thoughtful book on the psychological and anthropological importance of "home." Of course, Pope Francis's wonderful *Encyclical on Climate Change and Inequality: On Care for Our Common Home* or *Laudato si'* shifted the moral landscape of the Roman Catholic Church (and other faith communities, as well) with respect to Ecology and Creation.

I appreciated what I found about the importance of stories in Thomas King's 2003 Massey

Lectures *The Truth About Stories: A Native Narrative* (Toronto: Anansi, 2003) and *The Earth's Blanket: Traditional Teachings for Sustainable Living* by Nancy J. Turner (Vancouver: Douglas & McIntyre, 2005).

There is much food for thought in William McDonough and Michael Braungart's *The Upcycle: Beyond Sustainability – Designing for Abundance* (New York: Melcher Media, 2013) and in Michael Lewis and Pat Conaty's *The Resilience Imperative: Cooperative Transitions to a Steady-State Economy* (Gabriola Island: New Society, 2012).

For inspiration, especially when I get bogged down by life and lose sight of the stars, I continue to turn to the various works of Thomas Berry. It was also worth going "back to the future" to reread Bill McKibben's updated classic *The End of Nature* (New York: Random House, 2006).

For the gastronomical goof from *The Joy of Cooking*, I point you to the First Plume Printing in November 1973, a reprint of the 1964 edition, on page 373: "To boil or poach lobster for hot facility-type table service, put a folded towel on the bottom of a large, heavy pan. Place on it a 1 ½ to 2 ½ lb. live lobster. Cover with cold sea or salted water. Bring the water to a boil and cook for 5 minutes. Reduce the heat and simmer for 15 minutes, slightly less if the lobsters have recently shed and are soft. Drain. Serve at once."

About the author

Peter Denton is the author of three books in the RMB manifesto series: *Gift Ecology* (RMB, 2012), *Technology and Sustainability* (RMB, 2014) and *Live Close to Home* (RMB, 2016). He has been teaching interdisciplinary variations on the theme of technology, ethics and sustainability across Canada for 30 years. He is an activist, writer, editor, speaker and consultant, as well as an ordained minister of the United Church of Canada. He is involved in several volunteer roles with the United Nations Environment Programme, both as a civil society representative and as a contributor to UNEP's latest Global Environmental Outlook, GEO 6. Peter chairs the policy committee of the Green Action Centre in Winnipeg. He lives in rural Manitoba.

The RMB *manifestos*
PASSIONATE. PROVOCATIVE. POPULIST.

RMB has created one of the most unique non-fiction series in Canadian publishing. The books in this collection are meant to be literary, critical and cultural studies that are provocative, passionate and populist in nature. The goal is to encourage debate and help facilitate positive change whenever and wherever possible. Books in this uniquely packaged hardcover series are limited to a length of 20,000–25,000 words. They're enlightening to read and attractive to hold.

Gift Ecology
Reimagining a Sustainable World

Peter Denton

ISBN 9781927330401

Technology and Sustainability

Peter Denton

ISBN 9781771600392

An Altar in the Wilderness

Kaleeg Hainsworth

ISBN 9781771600361

The Earth Manifesto

Saving Nature with Engaged Ecology

David Tracey

ISBN 9781927330890

Digging the City

An Urban Agriculture Manifesto

Rhona McAdam

ISBN 9781927330210

The Weekender Effect

Hyperdevelopment in Mountain Towns

Robert William Sandford

ISBN 9781897522103

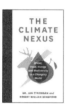

The Climate Nexus

Water, Food, Energy and Biodiversity in a
Changing World

Jon O'Riordan & Robert William Sandford

ISBN 9781771601429

North America in the Anthropocene

Robert William Sandford

ISBN 9781771601801

Denying the Source

The Crisis of First Nations Water Rights

Merrell-Ann S. Phare

ISBN 9781897522615

The Incomparable Honeybee

and the Economics of Pollination
Revised & Updated

Dr. Reese Halter

ISBN 9781926855653

The Insatiable Bark Beetle

Dr. Reese Halter

ISBN 9781926855677

The Beaver Manifesto

Glynnis Hood

ISBN 9781926855585

The Homeward Wolf

Kevin Van Tighem

ISBN 9781927330838

The Grizzly Manifesto

In Defence of the Great Bear

Jeff Gailus

ISBN 9781897522837

Saving Lake Winnipeg

Robert William Sandford

ISBN 9781927330869

Ethical Water

Learning To Value What Matters Most

Robert William Sandford & Merrell-Ann S. Phare

ISBN 9781926855707

Flood Forecast

Climate Risk and Resiliency in Canada

Kerry Freek & Robert William Sandford

ISBN 9781771600040

The Columbia River Treaty

A Primer

Robert William Sandford,
Deborah Harford & Jon O'Riordan

ISBN 9781771600422

Little Black Lies

Corporate and Political Spin
in the Global War for Oil

Jeff Gailus

ISBN 9781926855684

On Fracking

C. Alexia Lane

ISBN 9781927330807

Becoming Water

Glaciers in a Warming World

Mike Demuth

ISBN 9781926855721

RMB saved the following resources by printing the pages of this book on chlorine-free paper made with 100 per cent post-consumer waste:

Trees · 8, fully grown

Water · 3,680 gallons

Energy · 4 million BTUs

Solid Waste · 246 pounds

Greenhouse Gases · 678 pounds

CALCULATIONS BASED ON RESEARCH BY ENVIRONMENTAL DEFENSE AND THE PAPER TASK FORCE. MANUFACTURED AT FRIESENS CORPORATION.